AMERICAN VOICES

MEXICAN AMERICANS

AMERICAN VOICES

MEXICAN AMERICANS

by **Paula Lannert**

Rourke Corporation, Inc.
Vero Beach, Florida 32964

Cover photo: Greater Milwaukee Convention and Visitors Bureau

∞The paper used in this book conforms to the American National Standard for Permanence of Paper for
Printed Library Materials, Z39.48-1984.

Library of Congress Cataloging-in-Publication Data
Lannert, Paula, 1936-
    Mexican Americans/by Paula Lannert.
        p.   cm.—(American voices)
    Includes bibliographical references and index.
    Summary: Discusses Mexicans who have
immigrated to the United States, their reasons for
coming, where they have settled, and how they have
contributed to their new country.
    ISBN 0-86593-139-9
    1. Mexican Americans—Juvenile literature. 2.
Mexican Americans—Biography—Juvenile literature.
[1. Mexican Americans.] I. Title. II. Series.
E184.M5L313   1991   91-13125
973'.046872—dc20   CIP
                                               AC

CONTENTS

The Mexicans in North America 1
The Community 12
Mexico 21
Why America? 33
When They Came. 41
Where They Live 45
What They Do 54
Contributions to Society. 62
Famous Mexican Americans 71

Time Line. 83
Glossary 87
Resources 91
Bibliography. 93
Media Bibliography 95
Index. 99

AMERICAN VOICES

MEXICAN AMERICANS

THE MEXICANS

IN NORTH AMERICA

If, in the year 1848, a boy by the name of Juan Chávez and his family had lived in a town in what is now the state of California, he would have been living in Mexico. This would have been the case even though he had been born in that California town and had never traveled far from his family home. His Mexican nationality would have had nothing to do with his physical appearance or with the Spanish language that his family spoke. Juan would have been Mexican because California had not yet become a part of the United States of America—the territory which that state now occupies was then part of the nation of Mexico. A young boy named Daniel Smith might have been living at the same time in California, and although his appearance might have differed from Juan's and he might have spoken English, he, too, would have been Mexican.

One year later, in 1849, these boys would have been citizens of the United States, without having moved an inch from their homes. They and their families would probably not have made any change in their daily lives, but faraway conflicts over territory during the Mexican-American War had determined the future of their grandchildren. On February 2, 1848, those conflicts had culminated in a document known as the Treaty of Guadalupe Hidalgo. This treaty, signed at the end of war for territory, symbolized the beginning of peace and specified the transfer of millions of acres of land from the control of Mexico to that of the United States of America. What had been the northern part of Mexico now belonged to the United States, and eventually it would become Texas, New Mexico, Arizona, California, Colorado, Nevada, Utah, and Wyoming.

If, in 1848, Blasa Castillo and her family had been living south of the current border—say, in what is now the central plateau of Mexico—their citizenship would not have changed with the treaty. They would have remained Mexican. In a later time, perhaps, Blasa or her grandchildren might have felt compelled to travel a great distance north, cross a great river boundary, and become immigrants to a country whose landscape was familiar but which was, eventually, to seem foreign in ways that would seriously alter their lives. As immigrants to the southwestern United States, the Castillos would have become Mexican Americans.

WHAT'S IN A NAME?

It is difficult to imagine the southwestern United States today without the influence of the Mexican heritage. Although Mexican-American communities can be found throughout the United States, the largest concentration remains in the states that border Mexico, and the Mexican influence in that region, which less than two centuries ago belonged to Mexico, is profound.

But what, exactly, do we mean by "Mexican American"? This question is not always easy to answer—especially in the Southwest, where an invisible border between the two nations makes passage between them convenient and frequent. "Mexican American" refers to any citizen of the United States whose ancestors were born in Mexico. Mexican Americans are a unique group of "immigrants," because not all members of this group immigrated to the United States. Many who were residing in Alta (upper) Mexico in 1848 automatically became citizens of their new country. Others, driven by hardships at home, migrated from Mexico later. In both cases, Mexican Americans are sharply aware that they have inherited the customs and values of two cultures. This awareness has brought both joy and pain to a people whose identity and participation in American society continue to evolve and expand.

Many other labels have been applied to Mexican Americans, sometimes inaccurately or imprecisely. Mexican Americans are not "Mexicans"—that name refers to citizens of the nation of Mexico, not to Americans of Mexican ancestry. Similarly, Mexican Americans cannot be equated with "Hispanics," a name which refers to Spanish-speaking peoples in general. Although it is not inaccurate to include Mexican Americans *among* Hispanics, it must be remembered that those of Spanish, Cuban, Puerto Rican, and other Latin American ancestry are part of that group as well and have their own, unique cultures. "Latinos" is also used to refer to Americans of Latin American background, and therefore is not an exact term for Mexican Americans.

For a long time, a pejorative term for Mexican Americans (or Mexicans living in the United States) was "Chicano." This term was originally used by racist Americans who believed that Mexican peoples were beneath them. It may have derived from the mispronunciation of Mexicano as *meh•chee•cah'noh*. Then, in the 1950's and 1960's, during the rise of the Chicano movement—which advocated pride in ethnic identity—this term was reclaimed by Mexican Americans who wished to make clear to their fellow citizens that they valued their heritage and deserved the same respect as other Americans. Today, for some Mexican Americans, "Chicano" retains some of its former overtones, but many have embraced it as a positive identity.

3

Olvera Street, downtown Los Angeles, California, the center of the city's traditional Mexican-American crafts, foods, and culture.

SPANISH: AN AMERICAN LANGUAGE

What makes this group of Americans distinct? The Spanish language, either directly or indirectly, has done much to shape the cultural identities of several groups of Americans, including Cubans, Puerto Ricans, and other Latin American immigrants. The pervasiveness of Spanish as imported from Mexico shows that Mexican Americans are no exception.

For many Americans of Mexican heritage, English is the first and only language. Others grew up speaking Spanish but eagerly learned English, aware of its economic and political importance to their lives. A single Mexican-American family may contain members who speak mostly Spanish, mostly English, or both. The importance of the language to this group of Americans is evident in many aspects of daily life: Ballots and voting materials are published in both English and Spanish; television programs are often broadcast in both languages; newspapers serve Spanish-speaking communities; and instruction is given in Spanish as well as English in the many bilingual classrooms throughout North America.

Regardless of the individual exposure and use, Spanish has been called the soul of the Mexican-American culture, and the United States would be much poorer without its presence. What would Texas be like, for example, without its beautiful city of San Antonio (named for Saint Anthony) or California without Los Angeles (which means "the angels"), Sacramento ("sacrament"), or San Francisco ("Saint Francis")? The list of America's Spanish place-names numbers in the thousands, and the cities, towns, and regions that these names signify are now home not only to those whose ancestors were Mexican but to Americans of many other national origins as well.

THE CATHOLIC CHURCH

Since the earliest settlement of Mexico and the Southwest by Spanish missionaries, the Catholic Church has exerted an

Catholic cathedral in downtown Los Angeles, California: a center of Mexican-American religious life.

enormous influence on Mexican, and later Mexican-American, culture. The earliest missionaries established missions that became powerful and rich settlements. These missionaries converted the native Amerindian populations to Catholicism.

The Church remains a center of many Mexican-American communities, marking important occasions from baptism to marriage. Many of the dictates of the Catholic Church have continued to influence Mexican Americans to this day. Mexican Americans who embrace the Church have honored its policies concerning divorce or use of birth control, both of which the Church prohibits. Some Mexican Americans have broken from the Church or do not adhere to its strict rules, but Catholicism—so much a part of the culture of Mexican Americans and their forebears—continues to make its presence felt in the rituals and festivities that are such a central part of the Mexican-American lifestyle.

HOLIDAYS: RELIGIOUS AND HISTORICAL

The festive and colorful celebrations shared by the Mexican-American community with the public at large have served both to maintain a sense of community identity and to acquaint other Americans with the brilliance of the culture. Many of the festivals commemorate a time of religious significance; others celebrate the anniversary of an event important in the history of Mexico.

Religious *fiestas*, or holidays, such as the one held in San Juan Bautista, California, on December 14, often honor a saint. A particularly important holiday is the Festival of Our Lady of Guadalupe, which honors the patron saint of the Mexican people. Sometimes a unique occasion is commemorated in such celebrations: The Festival of the Bells, held in late July, honors the founding of the Mission San Diego de Alcala in San Diego, California. Other festivals, such as the Festival of the Flowers (celebrated in El Paso, Texas, before Labor Day),

7

take place all over the continent during all parts of the year.

Pageants called *posadas* (Spanish for "hotel" or "inn") reenact the efforts of Mary and Joseph to find lodging on the day when Mary gave birth to the Christ child. The *posada* is an especially important part of the Mexican Christmas celebration, and it continues to form part of the Christmas season for Mexican-American communities in *barrios* such as that of East Los Angeles.

Perhaps the most visible and important holiday among Americans of Mexican descent is a historical holiday, Cinco de Mayo, which celebrates Mexico's defeat of French troops on May 5, 1862. This occasion is a grand event in cities with large Mexican-American populations, such as Los Angeles and San Antonio, and is marked by parades, special foods, music, and dancing. In schools, children study the history behind the holiday and perform folk dances and songs.

Diez y Seis, which is the popular expression for "sixteenth of September," is Mexico's Independence Day, and it remains an important holiday to many Mexican Americans with close ties to Mexico. On September 16, Mexicans and those of Mexican heritage remember the same day in 1810, when *el grito*, "the cry" for the independence of Mexico from Spain, rose from the lips of Father Miguel Hidalgo y Costilla, one of the leaders of the revolt against Spanish rule. This speech, the equivalent of the American colonies' Declaration of Independence, is honored in Mexico and is widely celebrated in Mexican-American communities as well, from Toledo, Ohio, to San Diego, California.

FOODS FOR ALL OCCASIONS

No celebration would be complete without the tastes and aromas of good things to eat. The Mexican-American cook is capable of providing subtlety, drama, and excitement in the foods which he or she prepares, and as the palates of other

Greater Milwaukee Convention and Visitors Bureau

Children celebrate their Mexican heritage during the summer ethnic festivals in Milwaukee, Wisconsin.

Americans have become more sophisticated, they have come to appreciate the variety of fine dishes belonging to those of Mexican heritage.

The basic diet of Mexicans and many Mexican Americans includes tortillas (thin, flat, pancake-shaped bread made of cornmeal or flour and water), beans, rice, meat, various chilies, and seasonal items such as tomatoes (first grown by the Aztecs of Mexico), corn, squashes, and herbs. These ingredients are used to make everything from the typical restaurant versions of tamales (bits of meat encased in a cornmeal dough, rolled and wrapped in a corn husk and steamed), tacos (shredded meat and fresh, raw vegetables in a

9

tortilla shell), and enchiladas (chicken or beef and cheese wrapped in a soft tortilla and baked with a topping of chili gravy) to rib-sticking stews and pungent sauces.

A favorite of the Mexican-American gourmet is *mole* (moh'lay) sauce, served with turkey or chicken, especially at weddings. The sauce consists of four types of chili peppers, cinnamon, garlic, bananas, onions, peanuts, almonds, sesame seeds, raisins, cloves, black pepper, cumin seeds, coriander seeds, and chocolate, and it requires hours to prepare from scratch (groceries sell prepared *mole* for those who have less time). Another special dish, *barbacoa* (barbecue), is made by cooking a lamb or young goat (*cabrito*) whole for hours in an underground pit which has been lined with heated stones. The meat is cooked to a stage of succulence unlike that which any other method can provide. *Menudo* (made with tripe and hominy) is a stew or soup prepared by Mexicans and Mexican Americans on weekends and for festive occasions. Home-made tamales are often prepared during the Christmas season; they can be filled with sweetened mixtures of nuts, raisins, and shredded coconut as well as the more familiar meats. *Buñuelos*, fried rounds of sweet bread that are sprinkled with sugar and cinnamon, are also eaten during Christmastime.

AN AMERICAN VOICE

Like all Americans (with the possible exception of the Amerindians, who lived on the continent before the arrival of the Europeans), Mexican Americans have a mixed heritage. This heritage has solidified into an important group identity— especially since the Chicano movement begun by Reies López Tijerina during the 1950's and the farm-worker movement led by César Chávez in the 1960's. These activists protested exploitation of and prejudice against Mexican Americans and were considered radical by many Anglo Americans (and even some Mexican Americans), because they used social protest as a means of making the people's voice heard. Nevertheless, their activism paved the way for organizations such as the Mexican American Legal Defense and Educational Fund (MALDEF) and the Mexican American Political Association (MAPA).

Many of us group and name ourselves according to the place of our ancestry, for the sake of preserving those features of our heritage that bind us in constructive ways. At the same time, each American is an individual, a citizen of a nation called the United States of America. Whether or not we choose to identify ourselves with a group is a personal matter—there are no rules that say we must or must not do so. By studying our own ancestors and the ancestors of others, however, we can learn and gain an understanding about one another as individuals and as a people.

THE COMMUNITY

Whenever a particular group with a common heritage has emerged as a community abroad, its interests have been similar to those of any other group of immigrants, regardless of country of origin. Whether out of necessity or simply as a means of expressing their unique culture, members of most immigrant communities have expended some effort toward preserving the traditions of their parents and grandparents, maintaining close family and religious ties, and presenting a common front to the larger society. Not only have such efforts been demonstrated by Mexican Americans, but also circumstances have made it possible for this group—more so, perhaps, than any other—to establish and maintain a visible community.

"IMMIGRANTS" WHO NEVER LEFT HOME

When, in 1848, one-third of Mexico's northern territory was acquired by the United States as part of the peace agreement between the two countries—called the Treaty of Guadalupe Hidalgo—those who after one year remained in the ceded territories became citizens of the United States, regardless of their origin. Those who were Spanish-speaking, cultural Mexicans for the most part retained their old way of life; their immediate circumstances changed little, and so they had little need to change their routines. Those citizens of Mexico who, after 1848, began crossing their new northern border into what became the southwestern United States found established Mexican communities (now Mexican-American communities) in the chain of cities and towns with Spanish names which

Northern Mexico Before the Treaty of Guadalupe Hidalgo

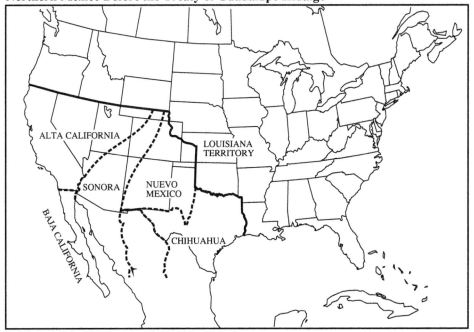

Territories After the Treaty of Guadalupe Hidalgo

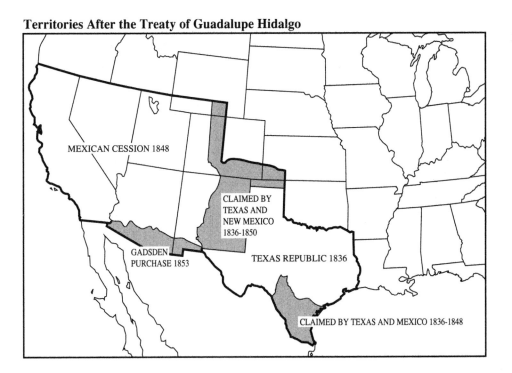

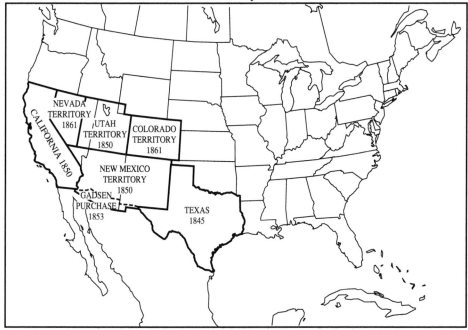

stretched from Texas to the California coast. These immigrants would have had reason to feel almost as if they had not left their home country at all.

No other group of immigrants has had the advantage of being so physically close to its homeland. New immigrants from Mexico have always had the option of returning to Mexico if things did not work out as planned or hoped. Moreover, because it is relatively easy to make temporary visits to Mexico, Mexican Americans have not been as geographically separated from family who remain in the mother country as have their European or Asian counterparts. The fact that trips are possible via land passage (as opposed to more expensive or time-consuming air or sea travel) has allowed Mexican Americans greater access to their loved ones.

Therefore, it has not been uncommon for some to return to Mexico to encourage family and friends to come and join them in the United States.

Likewise, the typical pressure to drop the mother tongue in favor of English has not been as great as for other immigrant groups—at least not in the Southwest, where Spanish has been entrenched in the region's culture since the sixteenth century. New immigrants from Mexico have continued to use Spanish in their daily lives. It has, in fact, been an advantage for those already established in the United States to be able to communicate in a common language with non-English-speaking immigrants from Mexico.

As a result of all these factors, Mexicans have continued to move to the United States in large numbers, reinforcing their cultural values among those already here.

COMMUNITY STABILITY

In the period between 1848 and 1910, Mexican Americans began to feel the first effects of industrialization. Economic development demanded cheap labor, and Mexican immigrants provided it. The newcomers, who were not yet firmly established, were dependent on others for jobs and housing, and they were often exploited by the *patrónes* (bosses) and others who sought good workers for subsistence-level wages. Urbanization was not yet necessary for those who spent seasons of each year in rural agricultural areas as migrant farm workers, and this factor kept external pressures from weakening the community.

It would have been far more difficult for many early immigrants to survive as newcomers in the United States had it not been for the assistance of those in their own community. Mexican Americans formed fraternal organizations, mutual aid societies known in Spanish as *mutualistas*, for the purpose of pooling their resources so as to provide loans as well as

15

temporary housing, food, and job assistance for Mexican immigrants who were in need. In addition, the *mutualistas* organized social events—fiestas and dances—and assisted families who were without resources during labor strikes. The source for the funds needed for financial aid and festivities came from monthly dues and occasional fund-raising events within the community. The formation of the *mutualistas* was along family lines, as were the trade unions, political action groups, and small businesses.

THE BARRIOS

In the cities, community stability was, initially, maintained because Mexican Americans were often forced to live in segregated and impoverished areas called *barrios*, where housing was substandard and neglectful landlords left their tenants in squalid conditions. Businesses in the *barrios* typically charged their Mexican-American patrons far more than the same commodities would cost in more prosperous neighborhoods. In rural *barrios*, Mexican immigrants often had to live in shacks made of whatever scraps of building materials were available: cardboard, bits of lumber, corrugated metal. Survival depended on close family and community ties, especially for those who did not yet know any English. Men from the *barrios* were constantly on the lookout for steady work in the fields, on railroads, or at construction sites.

Such conditions led to a cultural identity crisis among new generations of Mexican Americans. While the mothers and fathers retained their traditional Mexican domestic roles—men as wage earners and women as housewives who took on piece labor (often as seamstresses)—the offspring of these families were straining to form an identity for themselves as Mexican Americans. Teenagers who, because of their racial heritage had witnessed firsthand the hypocrisy of the American "dream" in the barrios, formed gangs and began a pattern of rebellious and destructive behavior that eventually fanned the flames of prejudice against their own people and wreaked havoc in the community at large. These *pachucos* were known by their unusual uniform, the "zoot suit," consisting of a long, shoulder-padded jacket and trousers that tapered at the ankles.

In the summer of 1943, rioting broke out in Los Angeles between *pachucos* and Anglo servicemen in the atmosphere of prejudice that had pervaded the trial of several Mexican-American youths wrongfully convicted of the murder of José Díaz near the "Sleepy Lagoon" swimming hole. Racism on the part of some Anglo police, journalists, and others was particularly obvious during this time. The zoot-suiter and the violence of the times were immortalized in Luis Valdez' 1978 play *Zoot Suit*.

By the 1960's and 1970's, the hopelessness of many Mexican Americans again led to rioting in such urban *barrios* as East Los Angeles and Santa Paula, as well as to the farm-worker and Chicano activism of this period. Mexican Americans were seeking not only the economic opportunities that had prompted their parents to immigrate; they also sought entry into the American society as *Mexican Americans*, rather than anglicized Mexicans.

THE FAMILY

Although urbanization and the pressures of modern living have done much to disrupt the traditional, close-knit family among Americans of all ancestries, the importance of the family in the Mexican-American community has remained strong. The family as an institution has helped define not only the personal and domestic lives of Mexican Americans but also their social, political, and economic identity wherever they have settled within the United States. Even as the twentieth century moves toward the twenty-first, Mexican-American families often live within short distances not only of

17

mothers, fathers, sisters, and brothers, but also of grandparents, aunts, uncles, cousins, nieces, and nephews. A sense of mutual responsibility and strong material and emotional support arise from such relationships and sustain community identity.

One manifestation of this key role of family has been the ritual of *compadrazgo*, "co-parenthood" or godparenthood. Partly religious and partly traditional in origin, the practice of selecting godparents for one's children has extended familial affection, so important in the Mexican-American community, and has been a source of emotional support for parents as well as for children. In times of crisis, displaced children have been accepted into the families of their godparents.

It is easy to understand why, given this rootedness in a family center, the Mexican-American community has enforced its strong identity in areas where large populations of these Americans have settled. The sense of family can be seen at the level of community groups and politics, in ethnic-pride movements such as *La Raza* ("the race," or "the people") and the Chicano movement, in labor organizations such as César Chávez' United Farm Workers of America, in civil rights groups such as MALDEF (the Mexican American Legal Defense and Educational Fund), and in performing arts companies such as Luis Valdez' Teatro Campesino.

A NEW PRIDE

All families and all communities have experienced the tensions and conflicts which occur when values are challenged in our fast-changing world. Mexican Americans, like all Americans, have felt the painful effects of industrialization and urbanization. The Mexican-American family is beginning to lose its once-enjoyed solidarity, especially in view of the trend toward intermarriage of members of its group with those of different heritages and the tendency of its young people to cast off the traditional male and female roles. Fewer Mexican

David Fowler

Mexican-American children play softball at a California school.

Americans today enjoy the benefits of the extended family home. Regrettable to some as it may be for the family to have lost many of its long-held values and traditions, there are those who believe that the close-knit, tradition-bound community has inhibited the assimilation of Mexican Americans into the larger society. Others would say that it is essential for Mexican Americans to maintain their cultural identity if they are to achieve the American dream. Whichever side is correct, the Mexican-American community has begun to thrive in the wake of World War II and the intense urbanization and enormous population growth which were its aftermath. This group of Americans has become such a huge force in the population, in fact, that the United States is expected to become the third-largest Spanish-speaking nation during the 1990's. It is no wonder that a new pride in Mexican-American identity is engendering this community's political and social revitalization.

MEXICO

Mexico is, above all else, a land of contrasts—in its geography, its history, and its people. Its topography includes a vast variety of landscapes; its people are a mixture of ancient Amerindians, Europeans, and Africans; and its history is both turbulent and politically unique.

LAND AND CLIMATE

Today, the nation of Mexico is about one-fourth the size of the United States, more than 750,000 square miles in area, making it the fourth largest in area among the countries of the Western Hemisphere. Its shape is somewhat like that of a cornucopia or horn. If one were to draw a straight line on the map of Mexico from the northernmost point, in Baja California, to the southernmost point, in the state of Chiapas, one would have measured a distance of almost 2,000 miles. The distances across Mexico from east to west range from 140 to 750 miles.

In the southeast, Mexico shares borders with the countries of Guatemala and Belize. Bordered on the east by the Gulf of Mexico and the Caribbean Sea, and on the west and south by the Pacific Ocean, Mexico has more than 6,000 miles of coastline.

Mexico's wide northern border is contiguous with the southern boundary of the United States, running along the edges of California, Arizona, New Mexico, and Texas. The Rio Grande—known in Mexico as the Rio Bravo (in Spanish, *rio* means "river, and *grande* and *bravo* describe the river as big, important, and formidable)—is, for part of its length, the

REGIONS OF MEXICO

BAJA CALIFORNIA

SONORA PLAINS

WESTERN SIERRA MADRE

NORTHERN HIGHLANDS

EASTERN SIERRA MADRE

GULF COASTAL PLAIN

SOUTHERN HIGHLANDS

VOLCANIC RANGE

SOUTHERN SIERRA MADRE

YUCATAN

CHIAPAS HIGHLANDS

NORTH AMERICA

dividing line between Mexico and the United States. The remainder of the border is defined by 276 international markers.

Immediately below the common border with Mexico are its two largest zones, which are bounded on the east, west, and south by the respective escarpments of the range of mountains known to Mexicans as the Sierra Madre, or Mother Range. (The northward extension of these mountains into the central United States is known as the Rockies.) These two zones, the northern and the central (or southern) highlands, constitute the main body of Mexico. Here, altitudes range from 3,000 feet above sea level near the border with the United States to heights of 8,000 and 9,000 feet in the central zone in and around the capital, Mexico City. Farther south, snow-covered volcanic peaks reach heights greater than 18,000 feet.

MEXICO

States (Estados)

1a Baja California Sur	12 Aguascalientes	
1b Baja California Norte	13 Jalisco	
	14 Guanajuato	
2 Sonora	15 Querétaro	
3 Chihuahua	16 Hidalgo	
4 Sinaloa	17 Colima	
5 Durango	18 Michoacán	
6 Coahuila	19 México	
7 Nuevo León	20 Morelos	
8 Zacatecas	21 Tlaxcala	26 Chiapas
9 San Luis Potosí	22 Puebla	27 Tabasco
10 Tamaulipas	23 Veracruz	28 Campeche
11 Nayarit	24 Guerrero	29 Yucatán
	25 Oaxaca	30 Quintana Roo

D.F. Distrito Federal (Federal District)

A wide coastal plain lies between the eastern Sierra Madre and the Gulf of Mexico and the Caribbean Sea. There are many excellent ports along the coast. While the area is subject to tropical storms, it contains rich farmland, oil and sulfur deposits, and forests of hardwood—some of Mexico's most important natural resources.

The narrow strip of land along the Pacific coast is less fertile and less productive, but it does have, along its shoreline, several fine harbors and many small fishing ports. Across the Gulf of California to the west of this area is the dry desert peninsula known as Baja (lower) California.

Below the southern Sierra Nevada are a narrow isthmus and the Chiapas Highlands, difficult to reach from the rest of Mexico until roads and a railway line were completed in the second half of the twentieth century. This is a region of strong contrasts: Here one finds pasturelands and mountain coffee plantations merging with tropical rain forests.

Temperatures in Mexico have more to do with altitude than latitude. In spite of its being the southernmost country in North America, almost half of Mexico lies more than 5,000 feet above sea level. While first-time visitors might expect tropical warmth and lush vegetation throughout the country, they soon discover, for example, that Mexico City, which is 734 road miles south of Laredo, Texas, lies in a desert valley some 7,350 feet above sea level (Denver, Colorado, is at 5,280 feet above sea level) and that it seldom sees temperatures below 48 or above 75 degrees Fahrenheit. In contrast, the town of Mexicali, just south of the California border, is one of the hottest places on earth, and summers can also be uncomfortably warm in the north-central highlands as well as in the coastal and southern lowlands. Rainfall in Mexico ranges from a few drops a year in the northern desert to an annual precipitation of more than 16 feet in the Grijalva River Valley in the state of Chiapas.

24

HISTORY
THE SPANISH CONQUEST

Upon the arrival of the Europeans (principally Spanish explorers) in the sixteenth century, Mexico was a land in which people had thrived for thousands of years. The records of a dozen or so pre-Hispanic Mexican civilizations show clearly that their achievements rivaled those of Europe, Asia, and Africa. The resident Aztecs (known also as the Mexica) were an advanced civilization, excelling in mathematics and related sciences as well as the arts and architecture, and they dazzled the Spaniards with what they had accomplished. By the time that the Spanish conqueror Hernán Cortés landed in 1519, the Aztec empire was a wealthy civilization: It had built aqueducts, causeways, pyramid-like temples, and other feats of engineering, and the famous Aztec calendar stone, twelve feet in diameter, was amazingly accurate and showed an advanced knowledge of astronomy. The Spaniard Bernal Díaz, upon first sight of the Aztec city of Tenochtitlán (today Mexico City), wrote: "Not even Venice [Italy] is richer or more beautiful."

Yet for all their admiration of this great native civilization, the Spaniards cared little for preserving its achievements and a great deal more for personal profit. The records of history have described the tragic end of the Aztecs. The Spaniards conquered these early Mexicans, brutally killing many in the process. Then, at the instruction of their leader Cortés, they forced physical (not necessarily cultural) integration of European expeditionary forces with those whose land and treasures Cortés now controlled in the name of Spain. The modern Mexican is a result of that integration, a mixture having come about through the marriages of Spanish soldiers with young women of the pre-Hispanic, conquered people. The Aztecs were deprived of their leaders, their priests, their cultural records, and their values, and were now dominated by strangers in their own land. It was with an understandable sense of loss of his own past that the character of the modern Mexican began to form.

In the years after the Spanish conquest, bad fortune did not escape the Mexicans, and with each succeeding tragic event, certain traits peculiar to the descendants of Cortés' men and their native tribes became magnified. These new Mexicans, neither European nor Amerindian and rejected by both groups, came to have a view of themselves as the outcasts or the underdogs who could only hope to come into their own one day.

FROM INDEPENDENCE TO REVOLUTION

In 1821, Mexico became independent from Spain, but as mistress of her own destiny, she had gotten off to a bad start. Having had no tradition of self-government, no experience in debate, no free elections, and not even the remnants of democratic institutions on which to build, Mexico was for the next hundred years either in turmoil or ruled by one or another foreign or domestic emperor or dictator. The border war with the United States in the mid-1840's ended in Mexico's defeat. Two decades later, it became Mexico's unpleasant task to rid herself, in 1867, of a French emperor. The subsequently elected president, Benito Juárez, was a Zapotec Indian who for years had struggled against the intruding Europeans and had occupied important government roles.

After the death of Juárez and a revolt against his successor, Mexico entered civil war. At the war's conclusion, General Porfirio Díaz became president in a virtually forced takeover in 1876. He proceeded to push the nation into its industrial revolution, and over the next thirty-four years, under his authoritarian regime, Mexico made rapid industrial and economic progress as a nation. President Díaz built extensive railroads, improved harbors, and increased trade. Large plantations produced an abundance of sugar, coffee, henequen,

U.S. troops landing at Vera Cruz during the Mexican-American War.

cotton, rubber, and tropical fruit. Steel mills and textile factories were expanded rapidly. American and European investment was welcomed. The nation's capital, Mexico City, became an impressive, European-style city of wide boulevards, parks, monuments dedicated to the heroism of former leaders, and palatial mansions.

Most Mexicans, however, benefitted very little from these improvements. Of the 10 million Mexican inhabitants, only a half million owned land. The remainder worked in virtual

serfdom. Under Díaz, much of what had been communal
farmland—which for centuries had provided a livelihood for
rural Mexicans—was sold. A few families (approximately
three thousand) owned more than half the land, and more than
half the oil fields and mines were owned by foreigners. Díaz
controlled the press. His rural police force was designed to
reduce the bandit traffic on the roads and highways, and it
made the roads safer in the early period of its existence.
However, many of the police were bandits themselves, and
they soon began committing crimes of rape and robbery
against the very people they were supposed to protect. With
no means of fighting the *rurales*, as the bandits-turned-police
were called, the peasants lived in fear.

When Díaz finally left office in 1910, a weak president took
over and rebellions started to flare up among the oppressed
people. Revolutionary leaders such as Emiliano Zapata,
Pancho Villa, and Venustiano Carranza began a period of
revolution that would last for many years. Toward the end of
that time, in 1917, a new constitution was written, guaranteeing
land reform, the right to organize labor unions, and free
education. A succession of rebel leaders acted as presidents
over the next several years.

REVOLUTION AS INSTITUTION

After the assassination of President Álvaro Obregón in
1928, the violence finally began to subside. The revolution was
not considered to be over. Instead, it was considered to an
ongoing march toward progress. Most Mexicans became
members of the National Revolutionary Party, which claimed
that it would put into effect the rights and reforms of the new
constitution. This party eventually had a monopoly on political
power; it was later modified by President Lázaro Cárdenas, in
1938, to include three sectors: peasant, labor, and "popular"
(unclassified workers, which eventually included the military).

Francisco "Pancho" Villa

Cárdenas was a very charismatic leader, revered among the Mexican people until his death in 1970. The country was still in poor economic shape, however. During World War II, Mexico and the United States became strong allies, making many agreements that benefitted both nations. After the war, a succession of presidents continued the effort to institutionalize the revolution and to bring about economic and social stability.

Although Mexico would have a new president every six years, as mandated by its constitution, and although its main political party would go through some changes, it would remain basically a one-party state. Some students of government see Mexico's government as a form of democracy, while others see it as an authoritarian system in which political action can be accomplished only by knowing the "right people." Economically, Mexico has seen great progress in many ways in recent decades, but there have also been setbacks. In the 1970's, it was anticipated that Mexico's booming oil industry would be the answer to poverty in that country. The Mexican government owned the oil, and because of the world's continued demand for petroleum, the revenues were expected to be extremely high and ongoing. Government planning was based on expectations of wealth rather than on sums already available. Unfortunately, amounts that were committed to be spent on government programs never materialized. The world oil glut in the late 1970's caused a sharp decline in Mexico's revenues. Perhaps worse, the number of available jobs in the oil industry and in supporting industries diminished. Those without skills who had anticipated oil-related employment or who had reason to expect the government to finance job training had few alternatives. Many looked to their northern neighbor, the United States.

Poverty has continued to drive vast numbers of rural Mexican citizens into the cities, where government services have been inadequate to prepare them for a new life-style. Mexico's high birth rate has contributed to the overpopulation of those areas where human beings can best thrive. Since the 1980's, there has been a surplus of labor over demand. Inflation has degraded the ability of rural, unskilled citizens to live in decent circumstances. All of these factors point toward continuing emigration to the United States.

THE PEOPLE

Mexico's population at the time that the Spaniards arrived in 1519 was a mixture of Amerindian peoples, including the ruling Aztecs. By 1800, the Indians totaled about half the population, and the other half consisted of European-born Spaniards (who held most of the power), American-born Spaniards, or *criollos* (the Spanish equivalent for "creoles"), and people of mixed blood: European-Amerindian (or *mestizos*) and European-African (*mulattos*). Today, Mexico's population is more than half mestizo, a bit less than a third Amerindian, and about 15 percent European.

Mexico's population has also changed from one that was largely rural (80 percent in 1910) to more than 70 percent urban. The central region of the country—especially in and around Mexico City—is home to a large portion of this population, and other urban centers account for significant numbers as well. Educational levels have also risen, although remaining low relative to the United States: In 1980, more than one-third (38 percent) of the population had no primary education, only 8 percent had some secondary education, and less than 5 percent had any postsecondary (college-level) education. As of 1985, less than a third of the households in Mexico had an automobile or a telephone, although nearly three-fourths had a television, and nearly all had radio. The preferred leisure activities were recorded as moviegoing, attending sporting events (including bullfights) and live theater, and visiting museums and national historical sites.

Although generalizations are often inaccurate, many aspects of the Mexican character can be seen as an outgrowth of the Mexicans' status as a conquered people. Racially, the modern Mexican is a product of the Spanish conquest nearly five centuries ago. Emotionally, the effects of conquest—by both Spain and, in 1848, the United States—can also be seen. Having been dominated (at least symbolically) by his European father and made to feel subservient by the conquerors of his mother's people, the new Mexican male offspring believed that he could never measure up to the image of his powerful father. The word *machismo* means "maleness" in Spanish, and the effort to prove his worth, his toughness, was for generations a primary pursuit of the Mexican man. *Machismo* became so much a part of the culture, in fact, that it influenced the structure of the social order. Differentiation between the strong and the weak was of great importance, and powerful leaders were often more admired than great ideals.

Less insecurity and more confidence is exhibited by more recent generations of Mexicans. A new, strong national pride has replaced the old feelings of wounding and rejection. The new Mexicans are comfortable with the fact that their history has been multicultural, and they are aware that, as a unique mixture, they are making outstanding contributions as world citizens.

WHY AMERICA?

The United States has long been seen as a haven for the oppressed and as a source of promise for those seeking a fair chance of achieving economic prosperity. To those living under totalitarian regimes or in nations where rigid class structures provide little or no possibility of upward mobility, the idea of "America" has offered a large measure of hope. The desire for economic opportunity and, at the extreme, the dream of vast riches have motivated many people from dozens of nations to move to the United States.

HOPE FOR PLENTY

After 1848, the first immigrants from Mexico to the United States (by then newly enlarged with the addition of the Southwest, formerly part of Mexico) had been inhabitants of their own border regions. Their proximity to the northern nation was important in their decision to migrate. Those living in the northern Mexican desert, near the borders with Texas, New Mexico, Arizona, and California, did not need to adjust to a different climate and topography, because the immigrants' destination was only a short distance northward, across the Rio Grande or across the imaginary line that marked the boundary between the two countries.

Some of the first Mexicans to become citizens of the United States by active relocation, as opposed to the annexation of 1848, were those who came soon afterward in the hope of collecting gold, which had been discovered in California. Stories of enormous quantities of the precious metal were a strong motivation for those who could endure the travel. When the Gold Rush was over, many of the approximately eight thousand Mexicans who had heard the rumors and followed the dream—only to be disappointed—stayed in California and entered the agricultural labor market or other enterprises.

The land boom, which came about as newly completed railroads brought easterners to the West and Southwest, resulted in more money-making activities and therefore more jobs. The abolition of slavery in 1865 meant that wage-paying jobs were available to Mexican laborers in the Texas cotton fields. California's produce and fruit had to be tended and harvested by hand. Men were needed to mine metals throughout the Southwest and salt in Texas. Mexico was a source of quality labor that was cheap and abundant, and so Mexican labor was actively recruited. Also, because of poor conditions in Mexico, larger and larger numbers of Mexicans were willing and anxious to cross their northern border in search of refuge from a hostile environment, as well as work.

FLIGHT FROM OPPRESSION

Toward the end of the nineteenth century, revolution in Mexico was becoming inevitable: The peasants were burdened with crime, with a rapid increase in population (Mexico's numbers rose by 50 percent between 1875 and 1910), with the failure of agriculture to meet demand (almost doubling food prices), and, for part of the period when the dictator Porfirio Díaz ruled (1876-1910), with an actual decrease in wages. Revolution broke out in 1910, and the violence would continue for many years. Motivated by hunger, the feeling of being helpless in their own country, and the desire to escape the civil disorder, unemployed Mexicans continued a steady northern movement that would last until 1929.

During the revolution and the subsequent years of strife in Mexico, a notable number of Mexican merchants, landowners, and intellectuals, many of whom had been displaced by the

34

war, came to Texas, New Mexico, and other areas in the Southwest for what was to have been temporary residency. Many of these refugees made the decision to remain in the United States, thereby becoming a part of the story of Mexican immigration.

In the mid-twentieth century, Mexico would begin irrigation projects, programs for mosquito control, and road building, but until that time, the greatest concentration of population was in the central highlands, an area providing a climate in which human beings are able to thrive. There, 25 percent of the people lived in 4.2 percent of the country's area. Most were engaged in agricultural production. From the three states immediately northwest of Mexico City (Jalisco, Guanajuato, and Michoacán) came large numbers of immigrants in the 1920's. While the land of this area is fertile and productive, it was then largely controlled by a small number of *terratenientes*, or "land holders," wealthy men who held huge estates. Most of the population earned wages as farm workers. As their numbers swelled and labor became too plentiful, it became necessary, periodically, for some to emigrate in order to find work so that they could feed their families. Fewer Mexican immigrants migrated from the coastal areas in search of work, probably because the periodic farm labor problem is less acute in the tropical zones.

THE DEPRESSION AND REPATRIATION

The Great Depression that began with the stock-market crash in October of 1929 was preceded by a decline in U.S. agriculture. Mexican immigration also declined as the demand for field labor diminished or was replaced by Anglo farm workers, who migrated west during the days of the Dust Bowl (when drought and dust storms plagued the Great Plains in the 1930's).

As a result, thousands of Mexican Americans were forced

from their jobs and began to leave the United States or to depend on government welfare programs. The Mexican workers who had been welcomed a few years before were now a burden, resented by the Anglos. Their Mexican heritage became a liability, and they were harassed and bullied. The governments of the United States and Mexico initiated a program of "repatriation" during which thousands of Mexican immigrants were transported back to Mexico. The problem, however, was not solved, only moved.

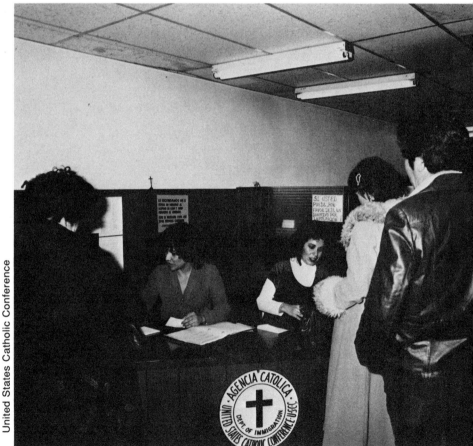

Two Mexican-American citizens take questions from long lines of immigration informatio seekers at the El Paso, Texas, office of the United States Catholic Conference.

THE BRACERO PROGRAM

In 1942, the United States government began a series of temporary contract-worker (*bracero*) programs. These programs were needed because, with the entrance of the United States into World War II in December of 1941, labor was once again in great demand. War industries were removing a large percentage of the labor force from agriculture. The *bracero* program was arranged by formal agreement with the Mexican government. Each Mexican worker was provided free transportation to and from his home, subsistence while in transit, and minimum guarantees as to wages and working conditions. The laborers were recruited by various farm organizations, which needed workers in order to plant, tend, and harvest their farm products.

Under the *bracero* program, Mexican nationals were able to work for wages that were far less than those paid to Mexican Americans, and they accepted substandard housing; the *braceros*, in effect, were indentured slaves. Still, their plight was not a bad as that of the "wetbacks"—illegal immigrants who crossed the border without documentation in order to find work. Both the *braceros* and the undocumented workers accepted severe poverty and mistreatment, but they were willing to suffer these inhumane conditions in the hope of attaining a better life for themselves and their loved ones back in Mexico, where the situation was hopeless. They also endured the prejudice of the Anglos and the disdain and resentment of Mexican Americans whose jobs they were taking.

The *bracero* program was suspended for a time after the end of World War II, but it had been so successful from the viewpoint of the employers that in 1951 it was reinstated. The program was popular with Mexican workers as well. Until the program was terminated at the end of 1964, almost 5 million workers entered the United States under the auspices of the *bracero* program. Many stayed and, with the aid of their employers, obtained resident status. However, a nearly equal (if not greater) number of undocumented immigrants were apprehended during this period.

IMMIGRATION TODAY

Immigration has continued to the present time in large numbers and in a steady stream from Mexico to the United States. Conditions and prospects in Mexico have improved, but not to the extent expected. Poverty, inflation, an increasing population, and a persistent unskilled labor force have continued to burden America's neighbor to the south.

The United States has therefore continued to hold forth hope for its neighbor to the south. Mexican citizens, despite a strong allegiance to their mother country, have recognized the opportunities available to the north and the need to provide for their families. Mexican mothers, for example—historically and to this day—have been so determined to provide their children with the chance for a better life that they have sometimes gone so far as to cross the U.S. border when the time came for their babies to be born. In doing so, they placed both themselves and their unborn children at great risk, but with the assistance of midwives, they delivered their babies in U.S. border towns, registered the births of their children in the United States, and then returned with them to their place of origin. As a result, these mothers secured for their offspring the right, when they reached the age of majority, to choose whether they would become Mexican or U.S. citizens.

Such motivation—strong enough to override any fear for personal safety—points to the ongoing uncertainties over the future of Mexico. Officials of the U.S. and Mexican governments are trying to find ways of increasing the economic opportunities open to Mexican citizens within their own country, but a large number of immigrants—some with

Mexican agriculture workers arrive by train in California.

and some without proper government documentation—
continue to pour into the United States from Mexico. The U.S.
Bureau of the Census has estimated that over the twenty-year
period between 1980 and the year 2000, the Mexican
immigrant labor force will have doubled, adding about 20
million workers. Because Mexico may not be able to provide
jobs in such numbers, many of these workers will have to go
elsewhere. The United States is their most likely destination.

   With agriculture still, at the beginning of the 1990's, the
largest industry in the United States, employing 20 percent of
the total work force, it appears that the demand for farm labor
will continue. Because travel between the United States and

Mexico is relatively easy and inexpensive, because many Mexican citizens have family or friends in the United States, and because living conditions in Mexico are poor and there are few opportunities for its citizens to meet their economic goals, the large numbers of Mexicans immigrating to the United States will probably also continue.

WHEN THEY CAME

The first Mexicans to become citizens of the United States were not immigrants. Texas' conversion to statehood in 1845, the large areas acquired as a result of a U.S. peace treaty with Mexico in 1848, and the Gadsden Purchase in 1853-1854 (which added the southern strips of Arizona and New Mexico) transferred to the United States a vast territory that had previously been northern Mexico. Each of these events caused the citizenship of the resident populations to change from Mexican to U.S.

Those who had been Mexicans did not always oppose the change, because the seat of their government was too far away for its northernmost citizens to enjoy Mexico's protection or even any regular contact. Still, the newly established border between the two countries did create the first Mexican "immigration" data. Official records of immigration were not kept until later, but it has been estimated that between 1845 and 1854, the area acquired from Mexico yielded the United States a Spanish-speaking citizenry of about 75,000.

Of these new citizens, approximately 60,000 lived in what is now New Mexico (some of these, at least, considered themselves to be of Spanish, rather than Mexican, descent); about 7,500 each were in what became California and Texas; and fewer than 1,000 were believed to be residents of what would eventually be the state of Arizona. Raids by resident Indian tribes had been so numerous and so frequent that Arizona was considered unsafe for scattered settlement.

The first large-scale waves of immigration occurred between

1910 and 1920. The massive arrivals during that decade were a reflection of both the expanding American demand for agricultural labor and the disruption in Mexico. Immigration slowed in the 1930's, a result of the worldwide depression of that decade and the ensuing program of repatriation (deportation) to Mexico. In the 1940's, 1950's, and early 1960's, when the *bracero* program was in effect, Mexicans were imported almost continuously. During the same time, illegal immigrants possibly outnumbered those "with papers." The total (legal, contract labor, and undocumented) was more than 7 million.

After the end of the *bracero* program in 1964, the steady rise in immigration continued. Immigrants arrived in large numbers because the economic conditions in Mexico were not good. Many of these immigrants were "undocumented." An undocumented (illegal) immigrant is one who is without documents of legal status. Such a person may be one who enters the country without inspection at a border. An undocumented immigrant may also be one who enters with the proper documentation for temporary status, but who later violates the terms of admission by allowing the expiration date to pass without applying to the proper authorities for extension.

The U.S. Immigration and Naturalization Service (INS) is responsible for preventing undocumented citizens of other nations from entering the United States. It is known that, in the past, large numbers of Mexican citizens have entered the United States without having obtained the required documents. The border between Mexico and the United States is, to many Mexicans, a "paper" border, formally acknowledged but physically "transparent," because the same physical geography appears on both sides of the international frontier; there is no major natural barrier, such as an ocean or an impassable mountain range, that hinders movement between the two

MEXICAN IMMIGRATION TO THE UNITED STATES, 1820-1989

Period	Legal Entrants Immigrants	Bracero	Undocumented Immigrants (apprehended)
1820	1		
1821-1830	4,817		
1831-1840	6,599		
1841-1850	3,271		
1851-1860	3,078		
1861-1870	2,191		
1871-1880	5,162		
1881-1890	1,913		
1891-1900	971		
1901-1910	49,642		
1911-1920	219,004		
1921-1930	459,287		48,503*
1931-1940	22,319		94,629
1941-1950	60,589	429,445***	1,322,142**
1951-1960	299,811	3,365,755	3,440,614
1961-1970	453,937	887,635****	1,027,193
1971-1980	640,294		4,847,131
1981-1989	975,657		

* For 1924 through 1930 only
** For 1941 and 1943 through 1950 only
*** For 1942 through 1950 only
**** For 1951 through 1967 only

Source: U.S. Immigration and Naturalization Service.

nations. Those who accept the reality of international borders and who are able to obtain the proper papers for entrance, residence, and employment, do so. Those who lack the information or the means for documentation and who choose to cross the border risk apprehension and deportation by the INS. The INS uses the number of apprehensions of illegal immigrants made by INS officers as a measure of illegal immigration. For example, INS data indicate that between October 1, 1988, and September 30, 1989, the number of people apprehended while trying to cross the southern border without the proper papers was 854,128. For the same period in the following year, the count was more than one million.

The Mexican birth rate has been high, causing great population pressures. Many Mexicans, desperate for work, will pay exorbitant sums to so-called *coyotes* ("smugglers"), who contract to bring them into the United States illegally. Once they have crossed the border, many obtain forged documents, such as Social Security cards, which can be used to obtain a U.S. driver's license. The larger and more widespread the crisis in their own country, the larger will be the numbers of Mexican immigrants to the United States.

WHERE THEY LIVE

Because the need for work has most often motivated Mexican immigrants, the rumored locations where labor is in demand, rather than considerations of climate and altitude, have determined their destination. Those Mexicans who have left the mild, dry highlands of their own country and have relocated to areas where temperatures are more extreme and/or humidity is greater (Texas' coastal regions and states such as Illinois, Indiana, and Michigan) have found it more difficult to adjust to the move and have often suffered from diseases to which the new environment has made them vulnerable. Those who, coming from the Mexican highlands, have settled in the Rocky Mountain states and farther west—areas which have a similar climate and well-entrenched Mexican-American populations—have fared better.

NEW MEXICO

On July 11, 1598, the first Spanish capital was established in what were then the northern provinces of Spain's territories in the New World. The settlement had to be moved more than once during its infancy, but the final site chosen was near what is now Santa Fe, today the capital of New Mexico. The settlement was made permanent through the efforts of its founder, Don Juan de Oñate, and the missionaries and colonists who had accompanied him on his long expedition north from within the interior of New Spain. An irrigation system was established in the settlement, so that agriculture could thrive. In addition, settlers began to raise stock, breeding them from the horses, sheep, and cattle that they had brought

45

with them.

Along the route followed by Oñate and his caravan, other major settlements sprang up. The Rio Grande provided water, and along the river's course, development began. The modern cities of El Paso (Texas), Albuquerque (New Mexico), and Taos (New Mexico, north of Santa Fe) saw their beginnings as centers of commerce between the new northern capital and its source of supply and authority many hundreds of miles to the south.

Interspersed among these towns were smaller communities, where a friar might have established a mission; there he would have tended a garden, raised a few sheep and cattle, and held Mass for a small number of settlers while he pursued the conversion to Catholicism of nearby Pueblo Indians, who were less hostile than the nomadic tribes to the west.

Life in the towns of New Mexico was simple. Adobe (earthen) huts or houses surrounded a central plaza. To the north, sheep, and, in the lower elevations, cattle grazed unrestricted. There were scattered fruit trees, vegetable gardens, a nearby stream or river, and a church-centered social life. For the most part, northern villages were communal and farming was cooperative. Irrigation was managed by a system of gated ditches; each landowner was given the water he needed for his acreage. (The hacienda system—with an owner who controlled many acres of land and hired workers to perform the necessary tasks—was more common in southern New Mexico.)

ARIZONA

The territory that is now the state of Arizona was, early in its settlement, part of New Mexico and was governed from Santa Fe. Missions in this area date back to 1692, but nomadic Indian tribes, who resisted conversion to the Catholic faith, actively and forcefully attempted to thwart Spain's colonization efforts, making it unsafe for settlers to live in remote areas. Most of the population was centered in the south, where presidios were built in order to withstand Apache attacks. The first such fortress was constructed at Tubac in 1752; another was built at Tucson in 1776. In the 1880's, the U.S. Army maintained a post in the area, responding to Indian raids and reducing the risk to miners.

Work in the silver and copper mines attracted miners from the Mexican state of Chihuahua, just across the border with Mexico. Already skilled and experienced in the techniques of mining, these Mexican workers (who called themselves *chihuahuitos*) played a major role in the development of industry. Many still live in what is now southern Arizona, where ties of language and culture helped to build strong communities. *Mutualistas* (mutual aid societies) sponsored social events and provided such material assistance as burial insurance. Mexican-American labor unions were eventually recognized, and they were successful in obtaining better wages, benefits, and working conditions for the miners.

TEXAS

In the late 1600's, Spaniards who explored the Rio Grande left a bull and a cow, a stallion and a mare at each crossing. Thirty years later, wild horses were running loose by the thousands and cattle were thick in the brush of what is now south Texas. Permanent Spanish missions and colonies were established at this time. Large stock ranches soon spread from the mission at Goliad down the San Antonio River.

It was near the tree-lined San Antonio River that the city by that name was founded, first as a mission, in May of 1718. Four more missions were built along the river during the subsequent thirteen years. Both Spain and Mexico have left their mark on modern San Antonio, which by the early 1990's had a population approaching one million—Mexican

MEXICAN IMMIGRANTS BY SELECTED METROPOLITAN STATISTICAL AREA OF INTENDED RESIDENCE

Metropolitan Statistical Area	Population Change for 10/1/88 through 9/30/89
Arizona	
Phoenix	3,961
California	
Los Angeles-Long Beach	149,827
Anaheim-Santa Ana	19,763
San Diego	13,794
San Francisco	3,800
Riverside-San Bernardino	14,668
San Jose	7,333
Oakland	3,671
Fresno	5,013
Oxnard-Ventura	3,602
Sacramento	1,101
Stockton	1,127
Bakersfield	2,402
Salinas-Seaside-Monterey	2,429
Visalia-Tulare-Porterville	2,535
Colorado	
Denver	1,884
Connecticut	
Bridgeport-Stamford-Norwalk-Danbury	31
Hartford-New Britain-Middletown-Bristol	21
Florida	
Miami-Hialeah	435
Fort Lauderdale-Hollywood-Pompano Beach	179
Tampa-St. Petersburg-Clearwater	526
West Palm Beach-Boca Raton-Delray Beach	260
Georgia	
Atlanta	612
Hawaii	
Honolulu	27
Illinois	
Chicago	32,541
Massachusetts	
Boston-Lawrence-Salem-Lowell-Brockton	93
Michigan	
Detroit	122

continued

Metropolitan Statistical Area	Population Change for 10/1/88 through 9/30/89
Minnesota	
Minneapolis-St. Paul	125
Nevada	
Las Vegas	1,381
New Jersey-Pennsylvania	
Newark	53
Bergen-Passaic	180
Philadelphia	97
Jersey City	61
Middlesex-Somerset-Hunterdon	50
New York	
New York	1,599
Nassau-Suffolk	78
Oregon	
Portland	290
Puerto Rico	
San Juan	42
Rhode Island	
Providence-Pawtucket-Woonsocket	32
Texas	
Houston	18,382
Dallas	9,499
El Paso	6,123
McAllen-Edinburg-Mission	8,787
San Antonio	5,344
Fort Worth-Arlington	3,995
Brownsville-Harlingen	3,699
Austin	2,640
Washington, D.C.-Maryland-Virginia	370
Washington	
Seattle	437
Other Metropolitan Statistical Areas	37,735
Non-Metropolitan Statistical Areas	32,416

Source: U.S. Immigration and Naturalization Service.

Americans making up by far the largest segment of its 55.59 percent Hispanic population.

The most heavily populated area of early Texas was in the towns—a series of trade centers along the Rio Grande. Among those was Laredo, founded as a ferry crossing in 1755, and El Paso, the westernmost. After the Civil War (1861-1865), cotton plantations moved into south Texas, where land had not been under cultivation and was cheap. Agricultural workers came into great demand as more and more Texas rangeland was converted to cotton farming, and Mexico was the best and nearest source for those workers. The Mexican-American population has since dominated the communities of the lower Rio Grande Valley, including Laredo, Harlingen, Edinburg, McAllen, and Mission.

CALIFORNIA

California's colonization was largely attributable to the Franciscan missionaries, through their efforts to convert the Indians of Alta (upper) California. Beginning in 1769, Spanish colonial policy began to establish a trail of missions, and around these missions the first towns developed. Many of these missions still stand. They serve as museums that provide the best evidence of the tranquil life that surrounded them.

Los Angeles, in southern California, was officially founded on September 4, 1781, when the Spanish governor of the territory marched to the site of the present city and declared it to be El Pueblo de Nuestra Señora, La Reina de Los Angeles de Porciuncula (The Town of Our Lady, the Queen of the Angels of Porciuncula), which has since been shortened to "Los Angeles." It was a sleepy little town until the mid-1840's, when it became part of the U.S. frontier. Its growth was stimulated by the Gold Rush (1849), and the completion of the railroads to the area (1885-1886) brought many new settlers. A land boom developed, and then came the discovery of oil.

Water was piped in from a nearby river in 1913, and the first major waves of immigration of Mexican citizens began soon thereafter. World War II and the rapid growth of war-related industries created a large demand for unskilled as well as skilled workers, and Mexican immigrants helped to fill those labor requirements. Currently, more people of Mexican ancestry live in Los Angeles than in any other city in the world, with the exceptions of Mexico City and Guadalajara in Mexico. Los Angeles continues to attract the largest number of immigrants to the United States from Mexico.

Throughout the territories that subsequently became known as the Southwest and West, settlements were established by Spanish colonial interests to be their trade centers or to be surrounded by their agricultural, ranching, or mining interests. The region's modern urban centers grew out of such settlements, which expanded with the growth of population. The names given to present-day towns and cities by their original Spanish settlers may even have encouraged later Mexican immigrants to live in and around such cities as San Diego, San Jose, and Los Angeles, providing a certain reassurance and a sense of having "come to the right place."

THE MIDWEST AND NORTHEAST

While most of those who have come from Mexico to live in the United States have settled and remained in the Southwest and the West, some have chosen the urban industrial centers of the Midwest and Northeast. By the early 1920's, many were being recruited by meat-packing plants in Chicago and Kansas City, others by Detroit's auto assembly lines, and still others by steel mills and by steel-related industries in Ohio and Pennsylvania.

It has been estimated that by 1930, about 15 percent of all Mexican Americans lived outside the Southwest. This was

SAMPLING OF STANDARD METROPOLITAN STATISTICAL AREAS HAVING POPULATIONS OF MEXICAN ORIGIN

Area	Population
Arizona	
Phoenix	177,546
Tucson	100,085
California	
Anaheim-Santa Ana-Garden Grove	232,472
Fresno	140,976
Los Angeles-Long Beach	1,650,934
Oxnard-Simi Valley-Ventura	100,629
Riverside-San Bernardino-Ontario	252,513
Sacramento	78,597
San Diego	227,943
San Francisco-Oakland	189,742
San Jose	176,838
Colorado	
Denver-Boulder	108,697
Florida	
Miami	13,238
Illinois	
Chicago	368,981
New Jersey	
Jersey City	1,385
Newark	3,677
New Mexico	
Albuquerque	71,617
New York	
Nassau-Suffolk	3,354
New York	26,332
Pennsylvania	
Philadelphia	8,535
Texas	
Brownsville-Harlingen-San Benito	138,509
Corpus Christi	151,126
Dallas-Fort Worth	223,105
El Paso	282,001
Houston	374,510
McAllen-Pharr-Edinburgh	221,971
San Antonio	447,416

Source: U.S. Bureau of the Census, 1980.

due, in part, to the fact that agricultural workers who were recruited directly from Mexico as well as from California, Texas, and other states migrated in patterns as they followed the various harvests. These trails took them into the nation's northern and eastern industrial areas. Many migrant agricultural workers settled in areas where they were able to find permanent employment.

Believing that life would be better in the cities than in the rural areas, large numbers of Mexican Americans migrated to urban centers in the decades after World War II. A mixture of rural and urban Mexican Americans settled in middle-sized cities: St. Paul, Minnesota; Kansas City, Kansas; Des Moines and Council Bluffs, Iowa; Grand Rapids, Michigan; Omaha and North Platte, Nebraska; Waukesha and Racine, Wisconsin; Toledo, Ohio; Kansas City, Missouri; and Fort Wayne, Indiana. Initial Mexican populations, having arrived in the 1920's to work in a variety of industries, have increased since the 1960's as a result of the resettlement of thousands of migrant workers.

WHAT THEY DO

Most people who leave their homeland to go to another country are searching for a better life. Sometimes the need is desperate: Stunning reminders appear in the troubling photographs and films that have recorded frightening scenes of Eastern Europeans attempting to claw their way to freedom over the Berlin Wall before it was opened on November 9, 1989. In the late 1980's, hundreds of thousands of Jews flocked to Israel once the Soviet government had softened its exit restrictions. These Soviets and Eastern Europeans, having made it to freedom, were faced with finding a means of earning a living in their new country, wherever it may have been. Many had been esteemed professionals in their motherland but had to settle for any work they could find once they were relocated. Often, manual labor was the only employment available to such newcomers, regardless of prior education, experience, or status.

For Mexicans—who have been crossing into the United States, in many cases with similar difficulty, for more than a hundred years—the same limited opportunities for employment have existed. Most immigrants have had to be willing to perform the jobs that the indigenous population finds least attractive but for which the demand remains high. Mexicans seeking work have formed one of the largest and steadiest immigrant streams, and they have filled their share and more of such jobs in the United States.

Today, Mexican Americans are engaged in every type of employment available in the United States. As they progress up the economic ladder, many are able and anxious to devote time to organizing and participating in activities and movements that in turn encourage the development of economic opportunity for Mexican Americans and, indirectly, for others. From the lowest-paid laborer to those who have served in the Cabinet of the President of the United States, Mexican Americans have greatly contributed to, and will continue to play important roles in, the development of America. The story of their employment has mirrored the United States' evolution from an agrarian to an industrial to a service-based economy.

WORKING THE LAND

Because Mexico, for much of its history since its independence from Spain in 1821, has had no middle class, most of its population has lived at poverty level and has had little hope for material security. The primary way to provide for one's family has been to earn wages as a farm worker, because 95 percent of the Mexican population has had neither the right nor the means to buy their own land. Drought, rapid population growth with its attendant oversupply of labor, and other causes of widespread hunger have often left Mexican citizens with no choice but to seek employment abroad. Knowing that on the northern side of the border there is great demand for agricultural workers and that these workers are paid many times what they could earn in Mexico, Mexicans have often crossed the invisible borderline as their only alternative to starvation.

After the Civil War, the United States needed laborers who would pick the soft, white bolls of cotton grown first in Texas and then in any area of the Southwest where water could be routed. Southern California's orchards, vineyards, and truck farms created an equally important demand for seasonal harvesters of these items. These individuals were largely exploited by their employers, who paid them low wages and worked them hard.

By the mid-twentieth century, Mexican-American agricultural workers were steadily being promoted to positions as recruiters, supervisors, straw bosses, equipment operators, repairmen, and clerks. Mexican Americans also provided services in the towns of the border states; their businesses included restaurants, rooming houses, retail shops, barber shops, drug stores, and grocery stores.

COWBOYS AND RANCH HANDS

While by far the largest numbers of Mexican immigrants have begun as agricultural workers, some of the earliest to immigrate were employed as cowboys, a vocation that inspired much of America's unique western folklore. After the peace treaty with Mexico in 1848 and the resulting amended border, great cattle ranches were established in the "new" south Texas. Experienced Mexican cowhands, known in Spanish as *vaqueros*, were hired to sort and work the cattle, and to drive huge herds to northern markets and to unstocked ranges farther west. The ranch owners and their Anglo workers learned the techniques of the immigrant *vaqueros*, whose impressive skills had been handed down for at least three hundred years. (As early as 1769, *vaqueros* had been active in the management of stock in what was to become the state of California.)

The first Spanish settlers had brought sheep to New Mexico in the sixteenth century. These sheep were the beginnings of herds which eventually numbered in the hundreds of thousands and which required the employment of many sheep herders and shearers. In Northern New Mexico today, there is still a rich tradition of sheep raising. The industries that use sheep by-products as raw materials include producers of clothing, blankets, and other items which are hand-woven and

Ranch hands at work in turn-of-the-century Texas.

constructed of the wool fiber from the sheep. These items are in great demand.

MINING: THE *CHIHUAHUITOS*

In the late nineteenth century, the *chihuahuitos* (experienced miners from the Mexican state of Chihuahua), immigrated to what became the state of Arizona. In spite of many difficulties, they were able to make a major contribution to an industry involving the dangerous sub-surface retrieval of valuable metal ores. Other Mexicans (notably from the Mexican state of Sonora, where silver had been mined since 1763) also came

north during the California Gold Rush in order to contribute
their experience as miners. Colorado, New Mexico, and Texas
benefitted from the labor and experience of miners from
Mexico.

BUILDING THE RAILROADS

Without the railroads, the rapid population and development
of the West would have been impossible. Much of the rail
construction was accomplished by Mexican labor, especially
along the southern desert routes. There, beginning in 1880, the
Southern Pacific (SP) and the Atchison, Topeka and Santa Fe
(AT&SF) lines were expanding. It was also at about this time
that the United States government limited Chinese
immigration, thus cutting off a major source of railroad
workers. Mexicans gradually replaced these workers,
ultimately making up the majority of those who laid track and
did the repair and maintenance work.

LEARNING NEW SKILLS

During World War I (1914-1918), Europeans were cut off
from travel to the United States. To take up the slack in the
absence of European workers, Mexican Americans were
recruited away from their traditional jobs in mining,
agriculture, and the railroads and into the skilled trades related
to the war effort. Learning that they were able to earn more in
these and other trades, many Mexican Americans, especially
those who had lived in the United States for a while and were
able to speak English, moved north.

They became machinists, coremakers, and mechanics in
factories that produced war material. In furniture
manufacturing, they performed as finishers and upholsterers.
They were painters and mechanics in industries that made
paint and chemicals and that refined and processed oil.
Mexican Americans worked as bookbinders and as press

workers in the printing business. In Ohio, Pennsylvania, and Illinois, they worked in meat-packing plants and steel mills. Women were recruited into the garment industry as cutters and seamstresses. Both men and women worked in California's canneries.

Mexican Americans who served in the military in World War II came home to take advantage of their well-earned government benefits. Some obtained a college education or learned new skills by attending trade or technical schools. Others bought land or started businesses. Those who had remained civilians during the war became skilled in war-related industries. Their skills were translatable to postwar use in such cities as Detroit, which drew workers to the automobile manufacture and assembly plants.

PROFESSIONALS AND ENTREPRENEURS

According to preliminary figures available from the 1990 U.S. Census, Mexican Americans continued to be overrepresented (relative to other groups) in low-skill occupations. Nevertheless, they made progress in obtaining secure and better-paying jobs, and their numbers in the professions—as college professors, teachers, librarians, accountants, lawyers, doctors, journalists, scientists, government and law enforcement officials, athletes, and entertainers—had increased.

Mexican Americans own and operate virtually every type of profit-making enterprise: industrial, manufacturing, banking, research, technological, engineering, design, construction, service, retail, wholesale, farming, and ranching businesses. Mexican-American entrepreneurs are newspaper and magazine publishers, restaurateurs, fashion designers, and manufacturers, packagers, and wholesalers of food products.

Mexican Americans whose families have been in the United States for several generations have been able to make real and

A toymaker from Laredo, Texas, at the Festival of American Folklife in Washington, D.C.

permanent gains, establishing themselves in the mainstream of the country's economy and society. Analysts of future employment opportunities in the United States expect that those with good communication skills in Spanish as well as in English will be in ever-increasing demand.

CONTRIBUTIONS TO

SOCIETY

The contributions and advances made by Mexican Americans, often in the face of great hardship and sometimes cruelty, are evident in all phases of life in this country. There have been earlier allusions to the hard, physical labor which Mexican immigrants have endured in order to earn their living—labor which involved mining the ore, tending and harvesting the crops, building the railroads and highways, and countless other endeavors which helped to put together the parts our country. More recent contributions made in government, business, and industry as well as in the literature and the arts have begun to enrich the cultural resources of the United States.

U.S. Senator from Hawaii Daniel K. Inouye has called the American culture a "pot of stew" rather than "melting pot." In a melting pot, everything has been combined into sameness, whereas in a stew, all the ingredients are still distinguishable in shape, color, texture, and flavor. Mexican Americans have offered their share of color, shape, texture, and flavor to the American "stew," and they have done so with a large amount of grace.

LANGUAGE

Beautiful, rhythmic Spanish is a mixture of all the tongues of all the peoples who inhabited that portion of the European

The Spanish and Mexican styles of architecture have shaped modern public and commercial buildings throughout the western and southwestern United States.

continent which evolved into the unique and independent country of Spain. It is fascinating to study the origins of Spanish words and proper names. As a Romance language, Spanish naturally owes much to the now-dead Latin language. Some words can also be traced to the earliest Spaniards (the Basques); others to the Phoenicians, Etruscans, and Celts; many to peoples of the earliest Jewish and Christian religions; some to the Greeks, the Carthaginians, and the Visigoths (Germanic); and more recently to the Arabic-speaking peoples.

Years would be required if one wished to master all the subtleties of the Spanish language. For daily communication, however, Spanish is not difficult to learn, because the rules of pronunciation are simple and direct, and the exceptions to the rules are few.

Considering that Mexico occupied the southwest quadrant of the United States in the first half of the nineteenth century, and that Spain's influence there extends even further back, it should not be surprising that English-speaking Americans have borrowed many words and expressions from their Spanish-speaking compatriots. The Spanish words brought into American culture by Mexican Americans have become most familiar as the place-names of rivers, valleys, mountains, states, counties, cities, towns, streets, roads, schools, and the like: from Santa Rosa to San Antonio, from the Sierra Nevada to the Rio Grande. We have only to look around us, especially in the Southwest and the West, to be aware of the many names that can be traced not only to Spanish explorers but also to the Mexican Americans whose influence played a part in the naming process.

Mexican Spanish has given rise to many common words as well as proper names: Often the inability of the borrower to pronounce or spell the Spanish properly made many of these words and phrases unrecognizable as Spanish expressions. Among the many Spanish words adapted into English are those used by Mexican immigrant-cowboys that were passed along to their English-speaking counterparts. The Spanish *la riata*, meaning "rope," was transformed to "lariat" by the Anglo cowboys. *Musteño*, meaning "wild horse," became "mustang"; *lazo* (slip knot) became "lasso"; and *vaquero* (cowhand) was twisted into "buckaroo."

The *vaquero* introduced not only the word *rodeo* but the event as well: Originally, the word described the periodic roundup, sorting, and branding of vast herds of cattle. After the roundup, a huge ball was held to celebrate the completion of the work. The modern American rodeo takes place in an arena where contestants compete for prize money. Events are designed to demonstrate the skill with which competing cowboys can ride, "break" wild horses, separate a calf from a small herd, rope and tie calves, and perform many other tasks that would be required of a modern cowboy or that typically would have been performed by the Mexican-American prototype.

While most of Mexico's inhabitants are fluent in the Spanish language, the Amerindian descendants of native cultures still speak many ancient tongues. There are more than two hundred of these Indian dialects, and sprinkled in the current language of Mexico are words that were originally used by the Yaqui, Tarascan, Mixtec, Mayan, and other tribes, with the Nahuatl language, spoken by the Aztecs, having had the greatest impact on the dominant Spanish. Many modern place-names in Mexico pre-date the Spanish influence. Examples are Chapultepec (grasshopper hill), the name of a famous park in Mexico City, and Popocatépetl (smoking mountain), a major volcano. The Nahuatl language also survives in words that are now part of English: *coyote, tomato, ocelot*, and *chocolate*, for example; in fact, many words ending in *-ate*, *-ote*, or *-ato* can be traced to Aztec roots.

Today, the language as spoken by Mexican Americans is

not precisely the same in all parts of the United States, nor is it always identical to that spoken by other Hispanics. Mexican Americans in Los Angeles have Spanish expressions of their own, as do those in South Texas.

MUSIC

The Mexican music that is most familiar to Anglo Americans today was largely European in origin, but pre-Hispanic Mexico was not without music; the flute and the drum were important instruments among the native Amerindians. Mexican-American music has borrowed from many cultures and has almost as wide a range of styles as does the music of North America in general.

The familiar music of the *mariachis*, musicians dressed in distinctive costumes, has an appeal outside the Mexican community because it is a hybrid and because of its festive nature. The mariachi band usually consists of several members, who stroll as they sing and play guitars, brass instruments, and violins. Mariachi music ranges from lively, upbeat brass sounds to *corridos* ("story songs") composed for guitar and voice. Band members dress in charro outfits, which were typically worn when similar bands entertained at the weddings of the French during the brief period in the early 1860's when these Europeans controlled Mexico. In fact, it is believed that the name *mariachi* (mah•ree•ah′chee) came from the French word *mariage*, which is pronounced almost the same way.

Another type of music that is popular among Mexican Americans, especially those of Texas (who call themselves *Tejanos*), is known as *música norteña* (northern music) by Mexicans and as *conjunto* by those in the United States and is associated with the northern border states. The singing— usually by two male voices accompanied by a small button-keyed accordion (perhaps introduced to the Mexican

66

Americans of South Texas by Czech and German immigrants in the late nineteenth century)—is reminiscent of polka music. *Música norteña* is considered to be the music of working-class *Tejanos*. By the 1990's, *norteña* had gained international appeal for those with an interest in "roots" music. Salsa, another popular musical style, combines the sounds of several Latin American regions into a sophisticated mixture of dance rhythms such as mambo, rumba, and merengue. Although salsa is not exclusively Mexican-American, it is embraced by many Mexican Americans as part of their larger Latin heritage. Salsa is associated with the music of Cuban performers Tito Puente and Celia Cruz.

The guitar is an instrument which was popularized by early Spaniards, and later Mexican immigrants, possibly those who worked cattle on ranches in South Texas, who may have been the first American singing cowboys. The guitar has gone from the solo instrument used to accompany the vocal expressions of a "lonesome cowpoke" to become a part of almost every type of American music.

FOOD

Today, it is difficult to imagine any American eating establishment that does not offer at least one item that originated from the cuisine of Mexican immigrants. The tortilla—the flat, round bread familiar in supermarkets and in combination with various meats and vegetables to make any number of specialty items—is almost as much a part of the United States' culture as is sliced bread. Mexican-American restaurants are familiar throughout the Southwest: in south Texas, where "Tex Mex" is the local descriptive term for the menu and where "chili" is a spicy meat "stew"; in northern New Mexico, where the diner is asked to choose between "red" or "green" sauce to be served with the meat or vegetables; and in California, where Mexican restaurants, of

Some typical Mexican-American dishes served in a restaurant (clockwise from upper left): tortilla chips, salsa, flan (a custard dessert), quesadillas, fajitas, taco, and enchilada; each plate also contains refried beans and Spanish rice, which accompany many meals.

various levels of authenticity, can be found in every town from San Diego to Sacramento. In fact, Mexican cooking has become so commercialized since the middle of the twentieth century that several national chains of fast-food restaurants have built their entire multi-million-dollar businesses on the popularity of Mexican cuisine. Mexican restaurants are now as common, and as "American," as pizza parlors.

SERVING COUNTRY AND COMMUNITY

The United States military has been greatly served by Mexican Americans, who during World War II were seventeen times awarded the most important medal the nation can bestow, the Congressional Medal of Honor—more than any other ethnic group. In 1942, at the Battle of Bataan in the Philippines, units of Mexican Americans, whose homes were in Arizona, New Mexico, and Texas, ably defended their post. Serving in the European theater of operations during World War II, an all-Mexican-American company, Company E of the 141st Regiment of the 36th Division (a Texas division), was one of the most decorated.

Mexican Americans served equally well in the wars fought in Vietnam and the Persian Gulf. Individual Mexican Americans in all branches of the service—including Marines, paratroopers, and tank corpsmen—have achieved outstanding feats in the completion of their respective missions, for which they have earned the respect of their fellows in the military as well as other American citizens. Upon the return of troops from the Persian Gulf in April of 1991, a large celebration was held for Mexican-American military personnel at Olvera Street in Los Angeles.

As the American experience has come to include active social movements, especially those that pursue solutions to the problems of minorities, it is important to point out the contributions which such activities have made toward the enlargement of participation by Mexican Americans in our system. An even greater achievement of such movements, perhaps, has been that U.S. citizens of all backgrounds have become more aware of the difficulties faced by individual Americans whose heritage is Mexican.

Handmade marionettes line a booth at Olvera Street, Los Angeles.

FAMOUS

MEXICAN AMERICANS

Hundreds of Mexican Americans have achieved national and worldwide celebrity, distinguishing themselves in virtually every field of endeavor. This chapter provides biographical sketches of a few who have received media attention and therefore may be familiar to young people. The list that appears at the end of the chapter contains the names of others whose contributions to their communities, to their nation, and to the world deserve our appreciation.

ACTOR EDWARD JAMES OLMOS

Edward James Olmos was born in 1947 in Boyle Heights, the heart of East Los Angeles, his parents having moved there from Mexico City after World War II. He was graduated from high school in Montebello and attended East Los Angeles City College, where he studied sociology and criminology.

Olmos began his career in 1961 as lead singer for a teenage rock-'n'-roll group called Edward James and the Pacific Ocean. From the mid-1960's until his first movie role in 1971, he worked as a nightclub entertainer, meanwhile developing his dramatic skills in workshops at the Lee Strasberg Institute and in experimental theater. During this time he also worked in episodes of television dramas such as *Kojak*, *Cannon*, *Hill Street Blues*, *Police Story*, *Hawaii Five-O*, and *Starsky and Hutch*. At the 1978 Cannes Film Festival, he won a Gold

Los Lobos, famous Mexican-American music group.

Medal for his performance in the film *Alambrista*. He won
numerous other prestigious awards as well, including a Tony
nomination for his 1978 performance as El Pachuco in the
stage version of *Zoot Suit*. Recipient of an Emmy award for
his performance as Inspector Castillo in the television series
Miami Vice, he was also praised for his lead performance in
the film *Stand and Deliver* (1988).

Olmos has devoted much of his time to speaking to young
people on the merits of discipline, determination, and
perseverance. In 1983, he received the National Council of La
Raza Rubén Salazar Award for Communication. He is highly
regarded as a spokesperson for the best that is Mexican-
American.

SINGER LINDA RONSTADT

Linda Ronstadt is of Mexican and German ancestry. She has
earned great acclaim and numerous awards (Grammy's,
platinum and gold albums and singles) as a singer not only of
soft-, folk-, and country-rock, but of period music and popular
ballads as well. Clearly interested in much more than the
development and use of her vocal instrument, her approach to
music has been intellectual. She successfully starred in the
Gilbert and Sullivan operetta *The Pirates of Penzance* in 1980,
and in Puccini's opera *La Bohème* in 1984, proving the depth
of her talent as well as demonstrating a desire to expand her
range of experience beyond that of a pop singer.

Born in Tucson in 1946, Ronstadt began in the 1980's to
reflect upon the richness of her Mexican heritage. Embarking
upon a serious study of the Mexican tradition of song as a
means of expressing feelings related to the events of life—
such as love, death, and revolution—she was a major
performer in the critically acclaimed television production
Corridos, created by Luis Valdez and first aired by the Public
Broadcasting System in 1987. Her album of ballads, *Canciones*

de mi Padre, has been widely acclaimed, and it was accompanied by a PBS program of the same name.

ARTIST AMADO M. PEÑA

Amado M. Peña, born in 1943 in Laredo, Texas, is an internationally known painter whose talent and ability were first noted and encouraged when he was in grade school. He obtained a master of arts degree in art and education in the late 1960's, but in 1979, after having taught art for several years at the high school level, he turned exclusively to painting.

Exhibitions and one-man shows quickly made the world aware that Peña possessed an extraordinary talent. His subject matter reflects his interest in the Southwest's Hispanic and Indian cultures and in the dramatic shades and tints of its deserts. He often paints families or women at work. His figures are sharply angular, and he makes use of repetition in order to suggest deliberate, rhythmic movement.

Skilled as a businessman as well as an artist, Peña owns several galleries, where he markets his own paintings and reproductions. He lends his name to many causes by producing dramatic posters, and reproductions of these posters, available throughout the United States, have given Americans as well as others the opportunity to know and appreciate in their own homes the unique art of this accomplished Mexican American.

SOCIAL CRITIC RICHARD RODRÍGUEZ

Controversial author, commentator, and social critic Richard Rodríguez was born in San Francisco, California, in 1944, a few years after his Mexican parents had settled there. The Rodríguez family spoke Spanish in their home and among their friends and family. The teachers at the school attended by Rodríguez and his siblings suggested to his parents that, for

Smithsonian Institution

Artisan Alejandro Gómez sculpts a head of Christ.

their children's sake, English should be the language of their home. Rodríguez gained confidence and succeeded in school after the family converted to English, but he missed the intimacy that was lost once Spanish was no longer the family's private language. He eventually developed his own theory, however, that while this cost had been high, without the sacrifice he might never have reached his potential.

Rodríguez opposes affirmative action and bilingual education. He urges members of minorities to accept themselves as Americans rather than as "foreigners" in the United States. Perhaps only by so doing, Rodríguez believes, can each enjoy the full benefit of membership in the society.

An outstanding scholar throughout his educational career, Rodríguez received his bachelor's degree in English from Stanford University in 1967 and his master's degree in philosophy from Columbia University two years later. He then worked for several years toward his doctorate in English at the University of California, Berkeley, followed by a year of study at the Warburg Institute in London on a Fulbright Fellowship.

Rodríguez's writings have appeared in *Harper's Magazine*, in the opinion and magazine sections of the *Los Angeles Times*, and in his work for the Pacific News Service, whose stories are selected for use in newspapers around the country. In 1990, Rodríguez completed documentaries about Mexico and Mexican immigrants for the British Broadcasting Corporation, and he was featured in two segments of the Bill Moyers series *A World of Ideas*, aired by the Public Broadcasting System in October of that year. Rodríguez' books *Hunger of Memory* (1981) and *Mexico's Children* (1991) are among the few written by a Mexican American to be accepted for publication by the larger New York publishing houses.

FOOTBALL STAR TOM FLORES

Tom Flores, whose father fled to the United States at age twelve in order to escape the horrors of revolution in Mexico, grew up to become both player and coach of a championship professional football team. Flores was born in Fresno, California, in 1937. In 1954 he was graduated from high school in Sanger, California, having starred on the school's baseball, basketball, and football teams. He was named Honorable Mention Junior College All-American in football while a student athlete at Fresno City College, where he earned an associate degree. In 1958, he earned a bachelor's degree in education from Stockton, California's College (now University) of the Pacific, where he had been selected for several All-American football teams.

Flores postponed for two seasons any effort to play professional football so as to allow time for full recovery of a shoulder injury, but in 1960 he joined the original Oakland Raiders football team. In his six years as quarterback with the Raiders, he completed 810 passes for 11,635 yards and 92 touchdowns. After two years in New York with the Buffalo Bills and two more with the Kansas City Chiefs, he was persuaded not to enter a business career when, in 1972, John Madden, head coach of the Oakland Raiders, offered him the position of receivers' coach on Flores' old team. The Raiders reached the playoffs six times and won the Super Bowl once during Flores' six seasons as an assistant coach.

Replacing Madden in 1979, Flores ably coached the team to another Super Bowl victory in the following year. Flores was named Coach of the Year in 1982, and the Raiders again won the Super Bowl in 1983. In 1984, the City of Los Angeles, where the Raiders had meanwhile relocated, honored Flores for his contribution to the city's image.

WAR HERO EVERETT ALVAREZ, JR.

Everett Alvarez, Jr., commander in the United States Navy, was born to farm-worker parents from Mexico in 1937 in Salinas, California, where he grew up. After high school, he attended Hartnell College and was graduated in 1960 with a bachelor's degree in electrical engineering from Santa Clara University.

On August 5, 1964, Alvarez' Skyhawk fighter plane was shot down over the Gulf of Tonkin during the Vietnam War. He was picked up by the Vietnamese and was held their prisoner for more than eight years. His was the longest captivity of the conflict. He later described these experiences in his autobiography, *Chained Eagle* (1989).

After his liberation and repatriation in 1973, Alvarez attended the Naval Post-Graduate School at Monterey, California, where he earned an advanced degree in systems analysis. He retired from the Navy in 1980 after a postgraduate term as Assistant Program Manager for the Naval Air Systems Command in the nation's capital. Also by 1980, he had completed a law degree, and subsequently he became associated with a firm of patent attorneys.

In 1981, Alvarez was appointed by President Ronald Reagan as Deputy Director of the Peace Corps, and shortly thereafter he accepted appointment as Deputy Administrator of the Veterans Administration. In 1987, he formed his own management consulting firm. He is in demand as a public speaker and serves on the boards of various public service organizations. Many projects, including parks, housing projects, and a school in his home town of Salinas, have been named for him. Among his many honors and awards are the Silver Star, two Legions of Merit, two Bronze Stars, two Purple Hearts, and the Distinguished Flying Cross.

KATHERINE D. ORTEGA, U.S. TREASURER

Katherine D. Ortega was born in a rural area of south-central New Mexico in 1934. The youngest of nine children, she showed a talent for mathematics and accounting even during her public schooling in Tularosa, New Mexico. She was graduated in 1957 from Eastern New Mexico State University at Portales with honors in business and economics.

With a sister, Ortega started her own accounting firm in Alamogordo, and she remained engaged in her business for about ten years. Moving to Los Angeles, she worked there for a time as a tax supervisor and as the vice president of a bank. In 1975, she was named director and president of the Santa Ana State Bank. She was honored by her alma mater in 1977 as Outstanding Alumna of the Year, and she has been the recipient of other honors, including the California Business Women's Achievement Award and the Damas de Comercio Outstanding Woman of the Year Award.

Ortega had been active politically since college, and she was appointed to several advisory positions by President Ronald Reagan. In September, 1983, she was appointed Treasurer of the United States, and the following year she delivered the keynote address at the Republican National Convention.

OTHER NOTABLE MEXICAN AMERICANS

Business
Fernando E. Cabeza de Baca
Solomón Luna
Antonio R. Sánchez, Sr.
Hilary Sandoval
Félix Tijerina

Education
Frank Angel, Jr.
Lupe Anguiano
John A. Aragón
Carlos E. Castañeda
Ernesto Galarza
Juan Gómez-Quiñones
Américo Paredes

Manuel Luján, Secretary of the U.S. Department of the Interior.

Engineering
José Andrés Chacón
Carlos Castañeda Villarreal

Entertainment
Juan A. Alonzo
Joan Baez
Vikki Carr
Peter Escovedo
"Lalo" Guerrero
Flaco Jimenez
Trini Lopez
Los Lobos (musical group)
Jorge Mester
Ricardo Montalbán
Anthony Quinn
Luis Valdez
Carmen Zapata

Fine Arts
Alfredo Mendoza Arreguin
Pedro Cervántez
Edward A. Chávez
Alejandro Gómez
Luis A. Jiménez
Michael J. López
Octavio Medellín
Manuel Neri
Michael Ponce de León
Porfirio Salinas

Government, Politics, and Activism
Juan Bautista Alvarado
Jerry Apodaca
Polly Baca-Barragán
Ezequiel Cabeza de Vaca
Raúl H. Castro
César Chávez
Dennis Chávez
Henry G. Cisneros
Benjamin Fernández
Octaviano Larrazolo
Manuel Luján
Solomón Luna
Gloria Molina
Roberto A. Mondragón
Joseph M. Montoya
Solomón P. Ortiz
Frederico Peña
Edward R. Roybal
Reies López Tijerina

Journalism and Publishing
Ronald F. Arías
Ignacio E. Lozano, Sr.
Philip D. Ortega y Gasca
Moisés Sandoval
Richard Vásquez

Literature
Oscar Zeta Acosta
Alberto Alurista
Rudolfo A. Anaya

Ronald F. Arias
Jimmy Baca
Raymond Barrio
José Antonio Burciaga
Rodolfo "Corky" Gonzáles
Rolando Hinojosa-Smith
Gary Soto
Estela Portillo Trambley
Tino Villanueva
Jose Antonio Villarreal

The Military
Roberto L. Cárdenas
Leo Márquez
Phil Valdez

Science and Medicine
Francisco Sánchez Alvarez

Luis Valentine Amador
Alonso Cristóbal Atencio
Francisco Bravo
Lauro F. Cavazos, Jr.
Héctor Pérez García
Lorenzo de Zavala

Sports
Robert Chacón
"Pancho" Gonzales
Efrén Herrera
Joe Kapp
Nancy López
Carlos Palomino
James Plunkett
Lee Trevino
Daniel Villanueva

TIME LINE

1519   The Spanish conquest of Mexico begins.

1521   Spain claims Mexico as its territory.

1810   On September 16, Father Miguel Hidalgo y Costilla leads a rebellion of Indians and demands a new government with a speech entitled "El Grito de Dolores" (the cry of Dolores).

1821   Mexico wins independence from Spain.

1829   Thirty thousand Anglo-Saxons and seven thousand Mexicans live in what was then northern Mexico (now Texas).

1830   Mexico attempts to limit the number of Anglo-Saxon colonists in Texas.

1836   Texas wins independence from Mexico and becomes the Republic of Texas (not recognized by Mexico).

1845   Texas attains U.S. statehood.

1846   Boundary, cultural, and economic disputes with Mexico lead to the Mexican-American War.

1848   The Treaty of Guadalupe Hidalgo ends the war between the United States and Mexico on February 2: The Rio Grande and the Gila River mark the southern U.S. boundary; earlier U.S. annexation of Texas is approved by Mexico; other territory is ceded to the United States in exchange for $15 million, and all inhabitants of these ceded territories become U.S. citizens if they do not choose to remain Mexican citizens after one year.

1849   Prospectors rush to California as word spreads that gold has been discovered there.

1850   California attains U.S. statehood.

1853   With the Gadsden Purchase, signed on December 30 and ratified the following year, the United States acquires from Mexico forty-four thousand acres, adding the Mesilla Valley to southern Arizona and New Mexico.

1861-   The United States is embroiled in civil war.
1865

1862 On May 5, Mexican rebel forces defeat the French. The event is later celebrated as Cinco de Mayo.

1867 Mexico is freed from French rule with the execution of Emperor Maximilian and the resumption of power by President Benito Juárez.

1876 Porfirio Díaz takes over as Mexico's president and begins three decades of authoritarian rule, during which Mexico becomes a developing nation but many continue to suffer ongoing poverty.

1880 The U.S. Census reports that 230,000 of its citizens are of Mexican origin or ancestry.

1880's Mexican workers migrate north for employment in Texas' cotton fields.

1882 The Chinese Exclusion Act opens the way for Mexican laborers to fill jobs previously occupied by Chinese.

1900 Mexicans are recruited to work on western U.S. railroad construction.

1900-1950 Mexican and Mexican-American labor predominates in southwestern agriculture, mining, and railroads.

1910 Mexico's revolution against the repressive regime of Porfirio Díaz begins.

1912 New Mexico and Arizona attain statehood.

1913 Migratory workers on a ranch near Wheatland, California, riot in protest against living and working conditions.

1914-1918 During World War I, Mexican Americans serve in the armed forces. Mexicans and Mexican Americans begin to relocate to Midwestern industrial areas, where they find permanent employment.

1916 New Mexico elects its first Mexican-American governor, Ezequiel Cabeza de Vaca.

1920 The U.S. Census records 486,000 Mexican-born persons and 252,000 American-born persons of Mexican parentage in the United States.

1924 Congress sets immigration quotas by country.

1929 The League of United Latin American Citizens (LULAC) is founded in Texas to keep the Spanish-speaking community informed of its rights and duties as American citizens.

1929-1939 The Great Depression strikes the United States. With fewer available jobs, Mexican immigration to the United States declines and masses of Mexicans return to Mexico.

1930	The U.S. Census reports that approximately 1,509,000 persons of Mexican ancestry live in the United States.

1930   The U.S. Census reports that approximately 1,509,000 persons of Mexican ancestry live in the United States.

1940   The U.S. Census reports approximately 1,571,000 of Mexican ancestry living in the United States (about half a million have been repatriated during the preceding decade).

1941-1945   During World War II, Mexican Americans receive recognition for extreme valor in the military.

1942   The *bracero* program begins. It will eventually import millions of Mexican nationals to replace laborers who are serving in the military and support industries.

1942   Police in Los Angeles arrest 300 Mexican-American gang members following the murder of a Mexican American near Sleepy Lagoon. The ensuing conviction of several gang members is reversed a year later and leads to the Zoot Suit Riots.

1948   Postwar activism in the Mexican-American community begins, resulting in the formation of Mexican-American activist organizations with political, social, and economic goals.

1949   Tennis champion "Pancho" Gonzáles wins the Wimbledon doubles crown with Frank Parker.

1950   The U.S. Census records the number of Americans of Mexican ancestry to be approximately 2,282,000.

1950-1953   Mexican Americans serve in the Korean War.

1951   The *bracero* program is extended and reorganized.

1953   Henry B. Gonzáles is the first Mexican American elected to the Texas state senate in more than a century.

Late 1950's   The Chicano movement begins to gain momentum.

1960   The Mexican-American population is estimated to be at 3,465,000 by the U.S. Census.

1960's   Mexican Americans are elected to political office in larger numbers than ever before.

1964   The *bracero* program ends.

1964   Joseph Montoya becomes the first Mexican American elected to the U.S. Senate.

1965   César Chávez leads grape pickers on a 300-mile march from Delano, California, to Sacramento, the state capital, to fight for better wages and working conditions.

1966   Reies López Tijerina, with members of the Alianza Federal de
        Mercedes, occupies the Echo Amphitheater in New Mexico and
        establishes a provisional government, in an attempt to reclaim
        land for a Chicano nation. He is convicted and sentenced to a
        two-year prison term.

1968   The Mexican American Legal Defense and Educational Fund
        (MALDEF) is founded.

1970   An estimated 6,186,000 Mexican Americans populate the
        United States, according to the Census.

1970's Mexican-American women begin to organize and to be heard.
        Mexican Americans hold positions as ambassadors, governors,
        and U.S. Treasurer.

1971   Golf champion Lee Trevino wins both the U.S. Open and the
        British Open.

1974   Jerry Apodaca is elected governor of New Mexico and Raúl
        Castro is elected governor of Arizona.

1979   Luis Valdez' *Zoot Suit* appears on Broadway.

1980   The U.S. Census records approximately 9,000,000 Americans of
        Mexican ancestry.

1980's Mexican Americans are first appointed to cabinet-level posts by
        Presidents Ronald Reagan and George Bush.

1981   Henry Cisneros is elected mayor of San Antonio, Texas, the
        first Mexican-American mayor of a major U.S. city.

1983   Katherine Ortega is appointed Treasurer of the United States.

1986   The Immigration Reform Act sets forth heavy fines for
        employers who hire illegal immigrants and grants amnesty to
        illegals who can prove residency since 1982.

GLOSSARY

Adobe: Sun-dried bricks made of mud and straw; also, a dwelling constructed of such bricks.

Alto, alta: Spanish for "upper" or "higher."

Amerindian: A native of the Americas before European migration in the fifteenth century.

Anglo: One of Anglo-Saxon ancestry; generalized to refer to any person of northern European ancestry.

Aztec: One of a dozen or more cultures of Mexico which flourished circa A.D. 1324-1521.

Bajo, baja: Spanish for "lower," "under," or "beneath."

Barbacoa: A method of cooking in which food (often meat) is wrapped and cooked slowly in a pit or hollow in the ground, surrounded with hot coals.

Barrio: An area, located within a city or town, that is inhabited primarily by those of a Spanish-speaking, or Hispanic, culture.

Bracero: A foreign worker admitted by international government agreement.

Cabrito: A young goat, or kid.

Californio: The name used to refer to the original residents of California.

Chapultepec: A grasshopper; also, the name of a hill in Mexico City, the name of a castle on that hill, and the name of the park in which each is located.

Charro: A horseman dressed in tight trousers, a short jacket, a wide-brimmed hat, and spurred boots; this costume is often ornamented with silver and trimmed with gold braid.

Chicano, chicana: Originally pejorative terms for a Mexican American or a Mexican (male or female) residing in the United States. Later transformed into a sympathetic term of identity for an American of Mexican ancestry.

Chihuahuito: A native of the state of Chihuahua, Mexico, who traveled north to become a miner in Arizona.

Chili: A pepper plant; also, the pepper which is the plant's fruit.

Cinco de Mayo: The fifth of May, on which Mexicans and Mexican Americans celebrate the defeat of the French forces on the same day in 1862.

Compadrazgo: Literally "co-parenthood," or godparenthood.

Conjunto: The name by which *música norteña* is commonly known in the United States.

Corrido: A "story song" performed to the accompaniment of guitars.

Coyote: A wild animal of the dog family; also, slang for one who, for a fee, smuggles undocumented immigrants into the United States from Mexico.

Criollo: A person of Spanish heritage born in the New World; the English equivalent is "creole."

Diez y Seis: Spanish for "sixteen." The Sixteenth of September, Mexico's Independence Day.

Enchilada: A rolled tortilla filled with meat and cheese, over which is served a sauce made with tomatoes and ground chilies.

Franciscan: One who belongs to the Catholic order of Franciscan monks, who came to New Spain in order to convert the aboriginal (Amerindian) populations to Christianity.

Frontera: Spanish for "frontier," "boundary," or "border."

Grande: Spanish for "big" or "great."

Grito: Literally, "cry." "El Grito de Dolores" ("The Cry of Dolores") is the title of a speech made by Father Miguel Hidalgo y Costilla in 1810, proclaiming Mexico's rebellion against Spain.

Hispanic: Anyone whose first language is Spanish or whose cultural traditions are identifiable, at least in part, as having been influenced by one's Spanish ancestry. Hispanics include Cubans, Salvadorans, Hondurans, Puerto Ricans, and others of Latin American or Spanish origin, as well as Mexicans.

Latino: A person of Latin American and/or Spanish-speaking background.

Lazo: Spanish for "knot" or "tie." This word gave rise to the modern cowboy term *lasso*, a rope tied in a loop and used to isolate and restrain cattle and other livestock.

Lobo: Spanish for "wolf."

Machismo: Literally, "maleness." The term refers to a value system among men which prizes toughness, stoic behavior, physical strength, and dominance.

Madre: Spanish for "mother." The term appears in many place-names in the southwestern United States.

Mariachi: A member of a band or ensemble of musicians dressed in charro costume who walk about a plaza, restaurant, or fiesta playing guitars, violins, trumpets, marimbas, and harps and serenading their audience with *corridos* and romantic ballads.

Mayan: An intellectually gifted culture that flourished in Mexico circa 1000 B.C. to A.D. 1546.

Mestizo: A person of mixed Spanish and Amerindian blood.

Milagro: Spanish for "miracle."

Mixtec: A Mexican culture that flourished circa A.D. 800-1521.

Mole: A sauce, often served over poultry, which combines many spices, chilies, and other ingredients—notably chocolate.

Musteño: Spanish for "wild horse." This term has entered English as *mustang.*

Mutualista: A mutual aid society, a fraternal organization designed to assist and support those in the Mexican-American community.

Norteña: A northerner; also used to refer to the music of the northern border areas.

Pachuco: A zoot-suiter.

Posada: Spanish for "inn" or "hotel." In Mexican and Mexican-American communities, the *posada* is a procession that symbolizes the search of Joseph and Mary for lodgings on Christmas Eve.

Presidio: A fortress.

Pueblo: A town or village.

Riata: Spanish for "rope." *La riata* became *lariat* in English, the rope used to isolate and restrain cattle.

Rodeo: A cattle roundup or exhibition of cowboy skills.

Rurales: The special police of the Díaz dictatorship in Mexico, who kept law and order in the rural areas by means of violence and terror.

Sierra: Spanish for "mountain range."

Taco: A dish consisting of a folded tortilla, sometimes deep-fried, stuffed with meat, beans, or cheese, and topped with chopped lettuce, tomatoes, and onions.

Tamale: A tube-shaped entree or snack item: meat surrounded by cornmeal dough, wrapped in a corn husk, and then steamed.

Tarascan: A tribe of the Aztec confederation.

Tejano: A Texan of Mexican ancestry.

Tenochtitlán: The capital city of the Aztecs of Mexico, today the site of Mexico City.

Terratenientes: Wealthy "land holders" who held huge estates in Mexico in the early part of the twentieth century.

Tortilla: The flat, round, pancake-like Amerindian bread made of flour and water or cornmeal and water, usually hand-shaped and baked on a hot, flat clay surface.

Vaquero: A cowboy. The Spanish was mispronounced by Anglo cowboys to become "buckaroo."

Wetback: A pejorative term for an undocumented immigrant who enters the country illegally.

Yaqui: A tribe of Indians of the borderlands of Chihuahua and Sonora, Mexico, believed to be related to the Apache.

Zoot-suiter: A Mexican-American youth during the 1940's who dressed in a clothing of extreme cut, called a zoot suit.

RESOURCES

For detailed information on the purposes, membership, and services of more than 370 organizations that serve or are composed mainly of Mexican Americans, consult *Chicano Organizations Directory* (1985), edited by Cesar Caballero (Neal-Schuman Publishers, Inc., 23 Leonard St., New York, New York 10013).

American G.I. Forum of the United States
3317 Manor Rd.
Austin, TX 78723
(512) 477-3222
   With approximately twenty thousand members, primarily of Mexican descent, this group exists to "perpetuate the principles of American democracy based on religious and political freedom for the individual and equal opportunity for all." It raises scholarships and conducts veterans' outreach activities, adult education, and economic development. Has state offices.

Association for the Advancement of Mexican Americans
204 Clifton St.
Houston, TX 77011
(713) 926-9491
   Sponsors educational, health, and social welfare programs to assist Mexican Americans. Also publishes a Spanish-language magazine.

League of United Latin American Citizens (LULAC)
900 E. Karen Ave., Suite C-215
Las Vegas, NV 89109
(702) 737-1240
   Established in 1929, this is the United States' oldest and largest Hispanic civic organization, sponsoring a wide array of outreach activities and social programs in education, housing, employment, and immigration rights.

LULAC National Educational Services Center
777 N. Capitol St., N.E., Suite 305
Washington, DC 20002
(202) 408-0060

This nonprofit organization, an offspring of LULAC, seeks to improve educational conditions for the Hispanic community in the United States. Offers scholarships and educational services.

Mexican American Legal Defense and Educational Fund (MALDEF)
634 S. Spring St., 11th Floor
Los Angeles, CA 90014
(213) 629-2512

MALDEF exists to protect the civil rights of Mexican Americans and has offices in major cities across the United States. The organization also raises scholarships, offers leadership training, and gives awards.

National Latino Communications Center
4401 Sunset Blvd.
Los Angeles, CA 90027
(213) 669-5083

A communications center that acquires, packages, and produces Latino programming that is seen nationwide. Also sponsors training, research and development grants, and internships.

BIBLIOGRAPHY

Catalano, Julie. *The Mexican Americans*. New York: Chelsea House, 1988. With an introduction by Senator Daniel Patrick Moynihan, this small volume for older children and young adults is heavily illustrated with both black-and-white and color photographs and covers the history of Mexicans in America from the sixteenth century to the present.

Coy, Harold. *Chicano Roots Go Deep*. New York: Dodd, Mead, 1975. The Mexican-American contribution in terms of effort, culture, tradition, and style is presented in an entertaining and sympathetic, yet objective, manner. In addition to an index and a bibliography, Coy offers a glossary including semi-English terms.

Galarza, Ernesto. *Barrio Boy*. Notre Dame, IN: University of Notre Dame Press, 1971. An autobiographical account, by this noted scholar and educator, of his childhood years in Mexico and, following his family's escape from the Mexican Revolution of 1910, of his experiences as a youth growing up in California. Spanish glossary.

Garver, Susan, and Paula McGuire. *Coming to North America: From Mexico, Cuba, and Puerto Rico*. New York: Delacorte Press, 1981. Part of a series on immigrants to America, this volume for the young adult audience benefits from generous quotations of eye-witness accounts of the immigrant experience. These quotations bring to life the daily hardships and prejudices faced by those who became Mexican Americans. Approximately 75 pages are devoted to Mexican Americans. Some of the black-and-white photographs grouped in the center of the volume illustrate the conditions under which Mexican farm laborers were forced to live and work.

Gomez, David F. *Somos Chicanos: Strangers in Our Own Land*. Boston: Beacon Press, 1973. Written near the height of the Chicano movement, this volume celebrates *La Raza* (the people) and documents their trials in an inhospitable Anglo society. Although the discussion clearly advocates a cause considered militant by some, it is well documented with footnotes and well indexed. A *vocabulario* (glossary) defines Spanish terms that have become associated with the Mexican-American experience. A thorough, if understandably biased, account of a key movement in Mexican-American history.

Gómez-Quiñones, Juan. *Chicano Politics: Reality and Promise, 1940-1990*. Albuquerque: University of New Mexico Press, 1990. Examines organizations and leadership that played important roles in shaping the Chicano movement.

Gonzáles, Rodolfo "Corky." *I Am Joaquin / Yo Soy Joaquin: An Epic Poem with a Chronology of People and Events in Mexican American History*. New York: Bantam, 1972. This long poem draws upon two thousand years of Mexican and U.S. history. Both English and Spanish text.

Meier, Matt S., and Feliciano Rivera, eds. *Dictionary of Mexican American History*. Westport, CT: Greenwood Press, 1981. Entries address individuals, institutions, developments, and organizations. Appendices include a chronology, a complete text of the Treaty of Guadalupe Hidalgo, a lexicon of frequently encountered terms, maps, and tables.

Miller, Tom. *On the Border*. New York: Harper & Row, 1981. The author traveled the two-thousand-mile length of the border between the United States and Mexico in order to understand and report on that unique strip of land, to which he refers as the "third country." Each chapter deals with a different town or city, its food, music, or folklore, its violence, its labor problems, or its industry.

Mora, Joseph Jacinto. *Californios: The Saga of the Hard-Riding Vaqueros, America's First Cowboys*. Garden City, NY: Doubleday, 1949. Documents the presence of Mexican cowboys in California in the eighteenth century. Illustrated by the author.

Morin, Raúl. *Among the Valiant: Mexican Americans in World War II and Korea*. Los Angeles: Borden Publishing Company, 1963. The more than 2 million Mexican Americans who served in the United States military during these two wars, including their heroics and the way they were treated, form the focus of this volume.

Pettit, Arthur G. *Images of the Mexican American in Fiction and Film*. College Station: Texas A&M University Press, 1980. Thoughtful analysis of Mexican-American stereotypes in popular American culture. Bibliographies list motion pictures, fiction, criticism, history, and ethnic relations. Indexed.

MEDIA BIBLIOGRAPHY

FILM

La Bamba (Columbia, 1987). Luis Valdez, director. Valdez documents the brief career of singer-songwriter Ritchie Valens (Richard Valenzuela), the son of Mexican-American migrant workers. Focuses on Valens' life and untimely death in a 1959 plane crash.

Chulas Fronteras (Brazos Films, 1976). Chris Strachwitz, producer. This musical sociohistory of life along the U.S.-Mexican border alternates sequences of Chicano music groups with scenes of daily life and special celebrations. The musicians discuss their music and what it means to them.

Death of a Gunfighter (Universal, 1969). Allen Smithee, director. John Saxon plays a strong-willed Mexican who puts himself between the Anglo and Mexican communities of the village where he lives.

High Noon (United Artists, 1952). Fred Zinnemann, director. Katy Jurado plays the strong Mexican mistress of Gary Cooper. Courageous and compassionate, she embodies the film's moral message.

The Magnificent Seven (United Artists, 1960). John Sturges, director. Charles Bronson plays a Mexican-Irish gunfighter, Bernardo O'Reilly, who dies defending the children of the Mexican town which he and his companions have agreed to protect from pillaging outlaws. At his death, O'Reilly affirms his Mexican heritage.

The Milagro Beanfield War (Universal, 1988). Robert Redford, director. A bean farmer in northern New Mexico stands up to and wins moral victory over Anglo land developers.

The Ox-Box Incident (Twentieth Century-Fox, 1942). William A. Wellman, director. Anthony Quinn, "The Mexican," dies with dignity in a story of mob rule.

Stand and Deliver (Warner Bros., 1988). Ramón Menendez, director. Edward James Olmos plays a tough, demanding teacher and inspires his Chicano students to pass advanced placement tests in calculus.

Valdez Is Coming (United Artists, 1971). Edwin Sherin, director. Burt

Lancaster plays Valdez, a Mexican-American deputy sheriff who is forced to confront a ruthless land baron over whom he eventually wins moral and physical victory.

Zoot Suit (Universal, 1981). Luis Valdez, director. This musical film, based on the events surround the Zoot Suit Riots in Los Angeles during the early 1940's, tells the story of a Mexican-American youth straddling two cultures. Edward James Olmos stars as the hip and macho El Pachuco, a mythic figure who directs the action throughout.

TELEVISION

Cortés, Ernie. Interview for *A World of Ideas with Bill Moyers*, programs 238 and 239 (Public Broadcasting System, 1990). Grass-roots organizer Cortés discusses current Mexican-American issues and his concern for the Chicano community.

"Los Mineros." Episode in *The American Experience* (Public Broadcasting System, 1991). This program documents the struggle of the miners who came from Mexico to assist in the development of the mines in Arizona.

Rodríguez, Richard. Interview for *A World of Ideas with Bill Moyers*, programs 232 and 233 (Public Broadcasting System, 1990). Rodríguez compares the Mexican and U.S. cultures.

MUSIC

Chulas Fronteras. Arhoolie Records, 1977. The sound track from the film of the same name (listed above). Written lyrics are included with the recording; songs include rural ballads (*corridos*) and country tunes.

Los Lobos. *How Will the Wolf Survive?* Warner Bros., 1984. Includes music such as *norteñas*, *corridos*, and rock 'n' roll. Played on authentic instruments by this group from the East Los Angeles area.

Los Lobos. *La Pistola y El Corazón*. Warner Bros., 1988. An album of traditional Mexican songs sung in Spanish and played on authentic acoustic instruments such as the *bajo sexto* and the *guítarrón*.

Paredes, Américo. *A Texas-Mexican Cancionero: Folksongs of the Lower Border*. Urbana: University of Illinois Press, 1958. An examination of the Texas-Mexican *cancionero*.

Peña, Manuel H. *The Texas-Mexican Conjunto: History of a Working Class Music*. Austin: University of Texas Press, 1985. Uses oral histories of musicians and radio industry personalities to examine the evolution of *conjunto* music since World War II.

Ronstadt, Linda. *Canciones de mi Padre.* Elektra Asylum Records, 1987. Rondstadt sings *rancheros, corridos,* and *charreadas* (music played in rodeos). All songs are sung in Spanish.

FICTION

Anaya, Rudolfo A. *Bless Me, Ultima.* Berkeley, CA: Quinto Sol, 1972. A story about a woman who is a mystic and *curandera,* and the forces of good and evil with which she must contend.

Anaya, Rudolfo A. *Heart of Aztlán.* Berkeley, CA: Editorial Justa, 1976. Teenaged Clemente is chosen by an old and blind fortune-teller to lead his people to the spiritual and temporal worlds of Aztlan.

Arias, Ronald F. *The Road to Tamazunchale.* Reno, NV: West Coast Poetry Revue, 1975. Revolves around the deathbed fantasies and musings of old Fausto, who prepares for death by inventing experiences that he could not have enjoyed during his life.

Bradford, Richard. *So Far from Heaven.* Philadelphia: J. B. Lippincott, 1973. A sendup of contemporary Mexican society which deliberately reverses the Anglo and Chicano stereotypes. Good-humored satire of race relations in the Southwest.

Chávez, Denise. *The Last of the Menu Girls.* Houston: Arte Público Press, 1986. The theme of this novel is the rites of passage into womanhood as experienced by Rocio.

Foster, Joseph O'Kane. *Stephana.* New York: Duell, Sloan, and Pearce, 1959. The heroine of this novel struggles to become part of the Anglo establishment.

García, Guy. *Skin Deep.* New York: Farrar, Straus & Giroux, 1988. A young Mexican-American Harvard graduate returns to the barrio, falls in love, and rediscovers his roots.

García, Lionel G. *A Shroud in the Family.* Houston: Arte Público Press, 1987. A contemporary family in Houston, Texas, experience social and political problems.

González, Genaro. *Rainbow's End.* Houston: Arte Público Press, 1988. Examines life in the lower Rio Grande valley in Texas as experienced by undocumented migrant workers during the 1940's and 1950's.

Hinojosa-Smith, Rolando. *Becky and Her Friends.* Houston: Arte Público Press, 1990. A modern Chicana searches for identity and independence.

Ponce, Mary Helen. *Taking Control.* Houston: Arte Público Press, 1987. Mexican-American characters are brought to life in this collection of short stories.

Taylor, Theodore. *Maldonado Miracle*. New York: Doubleday, 1973. Young José crosses the border illegally and joins a camp of migrant workers.

Trambley, Estela Portillo. *Rain of Scorpions and Other Writings*. Berkeley, CA: Tonatiuh International, 1975. A collection of short fiction written from the feminine perspective about strong, determined women.

Villarreal, José Antonio. *The Fifth Horseman*. Garden City, NY: Doubleday, 1974. A historical novel about the Mexican Revolution of 1910. The protagonist is a member of Pancho Villa's rebel forces.

Villaseñor, Edmund. *Macho!* New York: Bantam, 1973. A novel about a young Tarascan Indian who becomes a migrant farm worker.

INDEX

Abolition of slavery (effect on Mexican immigration), 34
Activists, 81
Adobe, 87
Adobe houses, 46
Albuquerque, New Mexico, 46
Alcalá, Mission de (San Diego), 7
Alvarez, Everett, Jr., 78
American dream, 33
American G.I. Forum of the United States, 91
Amerindians, 10, 31, 87
Anglo (defined), 87
Apodaca, Jerry, 86
Arizona, 41, 46, 84
Art, 74
Artists, 81
Association for the Advancement of Mexican Americans, 91
Aztec calendar stone, 25
Aztecs, 25, 65, 87

Bamba, La (film), 95
Barbacoa, 10, 87
Barrios, 16, 17, 87
Bautista, San Juan (fiesta), 7
Becky and Her Friends (novel by Rolando Hinojosa-Smith), 97
Bells, Festival of the, 7
Bless Me, Ultima (novel by Rudolfo A. Anaya), 97
Bracero (defined), 87

Bracero program, 37, 42, 85
Buñuelos, 10
Business leaders, 79

Cabeza de Vaca, Ezequiel, 84
Cabrito, 10, 87
California, 33, 41, 50, 83
Californio, 87
Canciones de mi Padre (album by Linda Ronstadt), 73, 97
Cárdenas, Lázaro, 28
Carranza, Venustiano, 28
Castro, Raúl, 86
Catholic Church, 5, 7
Chained Eagle (book by Everett Alvarez, Jr.), 78
Chapultepec, 87
Charro, 66, 87
Chávez, César, 10, 18, 85
Chiapas Highlands, 24
Chicago, Illinois, 51
Chicano (defined), 3, 87
Chicano movement, 3, 10, 86
Chihuahuitos, 47, 57, 87
Chili, 87
Chinese Exclusion Act, 84
Christmas season, 8, 10
Chulas Fronteras (film), 95
Chulas Fronteras (sound track), 96
Cinco de Mayo, 8, 84, 88
Cisneros, Henry, 86

Civil War (U.S.), 83
Compadrazgo (godparenthood), 18, 88
Company E, 141st Regiment, 69
Congressional Medal of Honor, 69
Conjunto (music), 66, 88
Constitution (Mexican), 28, 30
Corridos, 66, 88
Cortés, Hernán, 25
Cotton plantations, 50, 55
Cowboys, 56
Coyotes ("smugglers"), 44, 88
Criollos (creoles), 31, 88

Death of a Gunfighter (film), 95
Depression (1930's), 35, 42, 84
Detroit, Michigan, 51
Díaz, José, 17
Díaz, Porfirio, 26, 28, 34, 84
Diez y Seis, 8, 83, 88

East Los Angeles, 17
Educators, 79
El grito, 8, 83, 88
El Paso, Texas, 7, 46, 50
Enchiladas, 10, 88
Engineers, 81
Entertainers, 81
Entrepreneurs, 59

Family, Mexican-American, 17, 18
Farm-worker movement, 10
Farm workers, 15, 34, 50, 53, 55, 85
Fiestas, 7
Fifth Horseman, The (novel by José Antonio Villarreal), 98

Flores, Tom, 77
Flowers, Festival of the, 7
Food, 67
Franciscan (defined), 88
Franciscans, 50. *See also* Missionaries.
French in Mexico, 26, 84

Gadsden Purchase, 41, 83
Gangs, 16
Godparenthood, 18, 88
Gold Rush (California's), 34, 58, 83
Gonzáles, Henry B., 85
Gonzáles, "Pancho", 85
Government leaders, 81
Grito, El, 8, 83, 88
Guadalajara, 51
Guadalupe, Our Lady of (fiesta), 7
Guadalupe Hidalgo, Treaty of, 1, 12, 83

Heart of Aztlán (novel by Rudolfo A. Anaya), 97
Hidalgo y Costilla, Miguel, 8, 83
High Noon (film), 95
Hispanic (defined), 3, 88
Holidays (religious), 7
How Will the Wolf Survive? (Los Lobos), 96

Illegal immigrants. *See* Undocumented immigrants.
Illinois, 45
Immigration and Naturalization Service (INS), 42

Immigration from Mexico,
1845-1875, 33, 41; 1875-1910,
34; 1910-1920, 41; 1910-1929,
34; 1929-1941, 35; 1942-1964,
37; after 1964, 38, 42
Immigration Reform Act, 86
Independence (Mexico from
Spain), 26, 83
Indiana, 45
Industrialization, U.S., 15, 18
Industrialization of Mexico, 26, 35

Journalists, 81
Juárez, Benito, 26

Kansas, 51
Korean War, 85

La Raza, 18
Laredo, Texas, 50
Last of the Menu Girls, The (novel
by Denise Chavez), 97
Latinos (defined), 3, 88
League of United Latin American
Citizens (LULAC), 84, 91
Los Angeles, California, 50, 51
LULAC National Educational
Services Center, 92

Machismo, 32, 88
Macho! (novel by Edmund
Villasenor), 98
Magnificent Seven, The (film), 95
Maldonado Miracle (novel by
Theodore Taylor), 98
Mariachis, 66, 89
Mayan, 89
Menudo, 10

Mestizos, 31, 89
Mexica (Aztecs), 25
Mexican (defined), 3
Mexican American (defined), 2
Mexican American Legal Defense
and Educational Fund
(MALDEF), 11, 86, 92
Mexican-American War, 1, 83
Mexico, before 1848, 1; birth rate,
31, 44; climate, 24; education,
31; geography, 21, 23, 24;
history, 25, 26, 28, 30;
Independence Day (Diez y
Seis), 8; inflation, 31; modern,
31; oil industry, 30; people, 31,
32; poverty, 31; socioeconomic
levels, 31
Mexico City, 23, 25, 27, 51
Michigan, 45
Midwestern United States, 51
Milagro Bean Field War, The
(film), 95
Military leaders, 82
Miners, 57; in Arizona, 47, 57
Missionaries, 46, 47, 50
Missions, 7, 47, 50
Mixtec, 89
Mole, 10, 89
Montoya, Joseph, 85
Mulattos, 31
Music, 66
Música norteña, 66, 88
Mutual aid societies, 15, 47, 89
Mutualistas, 15, 47, 89

Nahuatl (Aztec) language, 65
National Revolutionary Party, 28
New Mexico, 41, 45, 84

Nortena (music), 67, 89
Northeastern United States, 51, 58

Obregón, Álvaro, 28
Occupations of Mexican
 Americans, 54
Ohio, 51
Oil industry in Mexico, 30
Olmos, Edward James, 71
Oñate, Juan de, 45
Ortega, Katherine D., 79, 86
Ox-Box Incident, The (film), 95

Pachucos, 17, 89
Painting, 74
Patrónes, 15
Peña, Amado M., 74
Pennsylvania, 51
Persian Gulf War, 69
Posadas, 8, 89
Poverty in Mexico, 30
Prejudice, 17
Professionals, 59

Railroads, 34, 50, 58
Rain of Scorpions (stories by
 Estela Portillo Trambley), 98
Rainbow's End (novel by Genaro
 Gonzalez), 97
Ranch hands, 56
Raza, La, 18
Repatriation (during 1930's), 36,
 42
Revolution, Mexican (1910), 28,
 34
Rio Bravo, 21
Rio Grande, 21, 46, 47, 50

Road to Tamazunchale, The (novel
 by Ron Arias), 97
Rodeo, 65, 89
Rodríguez, Richard, 74
Ronstadt, Linda, 73
Rurales (Mexican police), 28, 89

San Antonio, 47
San Diego, California, 7
Santa Fe, New Mexico, 45
Santa Paula, California, 17
Scientists, 82
Shroud in the Family, A (novel by
 Lionel G. Garcia), 97
Sierra Madre (mountain range), 23
Skin Deep (novel by Guy Garcia),
 97
"Sleepy Lagoon" murder, 17, 85
So Far from Heaven (novel by
 Richard Bradford), 97
Southwestern United States, 51
Spanish conquest (of Mexico), 25,
 32, 83
Spanish language, 5, 62; as
 American language, 5; place-
 names in U.S., 5, 64
Sports champions, 82
Stand and Deliver (film), 95
Stephana (novel by Joseph
 O'Kane Foster), 97

Tacos, 9, 89
Taking Control (stories by Mary
 Helen Ponce), 97
Tamales, 9, 10, 89
Taos, New Mexico, 46
Tarascan, 89

Teatro Campesino, 18
Tejanos, 67, 89
Tenochtitlán, 25, 89
Terratenientes ("land holders"),
    35, 89
Tex Mex (food), 67
Texas, 41, 45, 47, 83, 84;
    immigration to, 34
Tijerina, Reies López, 10, 86
Tortillas, 9, 67, 90
Treaty of Guadalupe Hidalgo, 1,
    12, 83
Trevino, Lee, 86

Undocumented immigrants, 37,
    42, 44
United Farm Workers of America,
    18
Urban migrants, 53

Valdez, Luis, 18, 73, 86

Valdez Is Coming (film), 95
Vaquero, 65, 90
Vietnam War, 69, 78
Villa, Pancho, 28

"Wetbacks" (undocumented
    workers), 37, 90
World War I, 58, 84
World War II, 59, 68, 85
Writers, 81

Yaqui, 90

Zapata, Emiliano, 28
Zoot Suit (film), 96
Zoot Suit (play by Luis Valdez),
    17, 73, 86
Zoot Suit Riots, 85
Zoot-suiters, 17, 89, 90